HEART SONGS

A HOLOCAUST MEMOIR

BARBARA GILFORD

ISBN 9789493056541 (ebook)

ISBN 9789493056534 (paperback)

ISBN 9789493056725 (hardback)

Publisher: Amsterdam Publishers, The Netherlands

info@amsterdampublishers.com

Holocaust Survivor True Stories WWII, Book 4

Cover photo: Clara Buchsbaum, Gretl Buchsbaum-Spitzer and Zuzana Spitzer

CONTENTS

For
David and Andrew
Asher and Elia
and those who come after

And in loving memory of my father,
who gave me this legacy

"Memory is a passion
no less powerful or pervasive than love.
It is the ability to live in more than one world,
to prevent the past from fading,
and to call upon the future to illuminate it."

Elie Wiesel
All Rivers Run to the Sea

RECOMMENDATIONS

Heart Songs - A Holocaust Memoir is enthralling, impossible to put down. It is a heart wrenching, poignant, and suspenseful story about Barbara Gilford's family - a family consumed by the Holocaust. Gilford makes us care deeply about the fate of everyone in the Buchsbaum family. You will marvel at Oma Clara's unimaginable tenacity, optimism, and boundless love. *Heart Songs* illustrates how bad decisions during the Holocaust could prove fatal. It also makes clear that high intelligence and foresight were not enough to survive the SS and the Gestapo. You had to be lucky. Gilford's poetic prose and trained psychological perceptions about Holocaust survivors and victims make for a compelling read. When you finish *Heart Songs, A Holocaust Memoir*, your heart aches to join with Gilford to mourn the loss of a family you never knew. Like Barbara Gilford, may we all "carry the Buchsbaums from Ostrava" with us.

Rabbi Stuart Gershon, D.D., Rabbi Emeritus, Temple Sinai, Summit, NJ

What a uniquely compelling story Barbara Gilford has brought to the much-needed canon of Holocaust memoirs. Starting with a discovery of letters, she takes us on a journey filled with her family's tragedies and triumphs during history's darkest days, finally emerging in the redeeming power of love, faith and memory.

Ken Shuldman, Author of *Jazz Survivor, The Story of Louis Bannet, Horn Player of Auschwitz*

* * *

Barbara Gilford's book, *Heart Songs - A Holocaust Memoir*, beautifully bridges the Holocaust story of her father, grandmother and Buchsbaum relatives and her own story, growing up in a family affected by the Holocaust. This is a story of love and loss. But it is also a story of longing: Gilford longs to embrace the family she never knew; she longs to have a conversation with her father about how he felt at critical points in the story she only learns after his death; she longs to claim a positive Jewish identity; and mostly she longs to tell the story of her relatives' lives and resilience. As she ends her book, "In the end, their lives and their individual, unique selves cannot be eclipsed by the tragedy and circumstances of their deaths. They exist together in life and in death and their memory lives on in our very cells and souls." Here, Gilford embodies the holiness of the Kaddish and the reader becomes part of the "congregation" that recites it with her.

Ann Saltzman, Ph.D., Emerita Professor of Psychology, Drew University, and Director Emerita, Center for Holocaust/Genocide Study, Drew University.

When an only child's imaginary friends include her unknown first cousin, Zuzana (Susi), and her unknown grandmother, Oma Clara, both lost in the Holocaust, we know we are about to read a heartfelt true story. But not only. This story is much, much more. This story sings because it's written by an extraordinary writer, a journalist with a passion for research, an artist with a passion for life, and a psychotherapist with a passion to know deeply the heart. *Heart Songs* takes us on an odyssey through the author's childhood, to her grandmother's last letters, to her father's monumental efforts to save his mother, to the weaving together of three generations whose legacy transcends their tragic deaths. *Heart Song*s is filled with longing, loss and grief, yes, but also enduring love.

Nancy S. Gorrell, Author, English Teacher, Director of the Holocaust Memorial and Education Center of the Shimon and Sara Birnbaum JCC of Bridgewater, New Jersey.

* * *

I was lucky to be sent and be able to read Gilford's book *Heart Songs - A Holocaust Memoir* even before its publication. It is a work of deep love and devotion, and a very well written one. It is rich in historical documentation, recreating the lost cultural milieu and the atmosphere of pre-war and pre-Shoah Moravian bourgeoisie.

I was most impressed with the author's burning desire to reconnect with the part of her roots she couldn't meet directly, especially her paternal grandmother Oma Clara. Clara stands out as a giant figure, an all-giving mother forever feeding even generations to come by way of immense love for her son. This love cascades through inscrutable channels onto the author, her family, and descendants. As Gilford tells us, "Children inhale information and become expert weathermen, taking the emotional temperature of the adults around them."

Reading the book, I could follow exactly the fusion and mingling between the author's wishful imagination and real feelings from her family transmitted to her since her birth (and perhaps earlier), and absorbed with the milk long before actually learning about the facts behind them.

Ferruccio Osimo, M.D., psychiatrist, IEDTA, Founder and Past President, Milan, Italy

INTRODUCTION

Morristown, New Jersey

Autumn 2014

I wasn't looking for treasure when, in a fit of cleaning, I lifted a stack of oversized books from the bottom shelf of an antique blue cupboard in my study. These books had been ignored and undusted for almost twenty years after I had moved them from my late parents' house. Nevertheless, they had stood as sentinels over an unknown and priceless inheritance. Between a world atlas and a book on Jewish history, I discovered a cardboard folder with disintegrating leather straps and corroded buckles. A frayed pink ribbon held it together.

The folder contained letters that my father's mother, my grandmother Clara, had written to my father between 1939 and 1941. I knew just enough German to understand they covered some of the missing years in my grandmother's brave but ultimately tragic story and to translate her yearning expressions of love for my father. It took all my self-control not to press the letters to my chest and let my tears stain my grandmother's fine script. I wanted to consume her words and bury myself in all those missing years.

Like many Jews, my grandmother had fled her home to escape the Nazi occupation. While I knew the ending of her story, I'd never known what happened after she left Ostrava, Czechoslovakia in 1939 except for one piece of information: "She fled to Italy." The letters ended in December 1941 when the United States entered World War II. Previously I'd known Clara only through photographs and my father's stories. With my discovery of these letters I could add her loving voice to the family history my father had written in the 1970s.

If I believed in destiny, I'd say those letters had waited for me my whole life. They came to me as I stood on the cusp of retiring as a psychotherapist. They had waited until I was old enough to appreciate them. As I held the packet, I felt a personal and historical imperative to write my Oma Clara's story of those missing years.

Immediately after discovering the collection, I realized I needed a translator. I could tell the letters covered not only my grandmother's story but those of my Great Uncle Norbert and my Aunt Gretl and Uncle Hugo Spitzer as well. Hugo and Norbert had written at length. Even Gretl and Hugo's daughter, my first cousin Zuzana (Susi), had appended notes to my father below her mother's signature.

The folder also contained official documents and a tantalizing place name: San Donato Val di Comino. The index of my well-worn world atlas did not contain this place.

I called the German departments of two local universities to find a translator. Neither answered. An institute in New York that collects and archives information on German-speaking Jews was only too eager, however. "Yes, yes, of course we will translate your letters," they said, "but we want the originals for our collection. No, we cannot make an exception to our policy."

A miraculous phone call from a former professional colleague solved the dilemma. Kerstin White, an old writing circle friend, is German by birth and upbringing, a Jungian therapist, and a poet and writer. She wanted to sublet office space from me. After we determined my office was too small for her needs, she came to my home for tea. There she offered to translate the letters.

My grandmother's small, precisely formed script, written on tissue-thin paper, did not daunt Kerstin. Neither did the large number of them, fifty-seven in all. I did not hesitate to give her the originals. I trusted in her knowledge of the written word. Even more, I trusted her gentleness, sensitivity, and the great respect she demonstrated for the letters.

After a few days Kerstin asked for guidance. "Barbara, you need to make a decision," she said. "I can translate the letters exactly as they are written, but I am hearing undertones, certain tensions."

"Kerstin, I trust your judgment," I replied. "Translate them as you think my grandmother intended."

I never doubted the rightness of that decision and have been immensely rewarded. Kerstin gave me my grandmother's voice and her many thoughts and feelings. She said she fell in love with my grandmother while translating her words.

The letters led me on an odyssey into Europe and my grandmother's heart that I never could have imagined. They carried me into my own nether regions where I continue to grieve the loss of something I never really had.

PROLOGUE

San Donato Val di Comino

August 2018

During World War II, twenty-eight Jewish refugees found sanctuary in the village of San Donato Val di Comino, interned by the Italian government while desperately awaiting visas to countries beyond Europe's borders.

On my journey there, the flat landscape gave way to gently rolling hills an hour east of Rome. As our car glided past dry, yellowing fields with red poppies, I leaned forward as if to propel the car to move faster. In the distance the Apennine mountain range offered a vista of green forests topped by craggy peaks.

The town's twisting, cobbled streets served as a fortress against invasion. There, the foreigners lived among Italians of singular courage and moral fiber. Those houses, those streets, those people held stories and information about my grandmother, Clara Buchsbaum, and twenty-seven others.

As we approached, red-tile roofs and medieval stone houses came into view against the dark green slope of a mountain. *I know this place.* Emerging from the mist of an old memory, I recalled a 1954 family trip to Italy. I was nine years old. My father had stopped our car and walked up a small hill. His gaze sought the contours of the stone houses in the distance. Sadness enveloped all of us. I thought the feeling might be connected to my father's family who had died in the war. I did not yet know how.

We stood silently, watching my father. He looked like a statue and seemed far away. *Are his lips moving?* I thought back then. *Is he reciting Kaddish for my Oma who lived here during the war? Are there tears in his eyes?* The tableau had lived inside me for more than sixty years.

Hans, who later anglicized his name to John and became my father, had miraculously found refuge in England and later in America. After the war, my father had advertised for information about his missing family. But that one day in 1954, he had stopped himself from going into the town. What had kept him from entering the last place his mother lived? Had he feared the power of his loss? Did he believe the weight of his grief could shatter him?

Entering the town with my sons David and Andrew, and David's wife, Shari, I felt past and present coalesce. Only minutes later, it seemed, we stood in front of Casa Gaudiello at 5 Via Orologio. This stately residence, once a hotel, was my Oma Clara's last home. It was the place where she had written those loving letters to her son who had escaped and to her daughter Gretl and granddaughter Susi, trapped back home in Ostrava, Czechoslovakia.

Where sixty years ago my father turned away, I kept going. I rested my cheek against the stone façade which surely held griefs more ancient than mine. My sadness felt familiar and small, just like me. I pressed my hands over my mouth, one on top of the other, to hold back a sob. *Whose grief is this? Am I mourning my loss of a family I never met?* It felt as if the salt of my tears could melt the stone and release long held secrets. *Did the stone sigh or was that me?*

In that moment the stone yielded to a kind of alchemy beneath my cheek, becoming both the portal to my grandmother's sanctuary and the grave marker she was ultimately denied.

I was in San Donato with my sons to find my grandmother and any vestiges of her presence there—a place that she had hoped would provide shelter, clean mountain air and a haven until she reunited with her precious children.

1 BEGINNINGS (1900-1939)

The City of Ostrava, in the province of Moravia, was the geographic center of the Buchsbaum family from 1900 until 1939. Up until 1918 and the World War I Armistice, Czechoslovakia was part of the Austro-Hungarian Empire. After 1918, Czechoslovakia became a democracy in which Czech was the official language.

My father referred to his home city as Mährisch Ostrau until he died in 1988, even though the city's name had become Moravská Ostrava in Czech. Both German and Czech were spoken but German was the language of the Buchsbaum family at home.

The pull of place for the Buchsbaum and Babad families, who lived within a thirty-mile radius of the city center, kept most of them rooted in the same corner of Czechoslovakia for generations, perhaps for hundreds of years. The romance and culture of Prague and Vienna, two very old and beautiful cities with illustrious histories, cities they visited frequently, even lived in during university and apprenticeship years, did not appear to compete with the familiarity and comfort of home. The two exceptions were Clara's brother Norbert, who attended the University of Vienna and practiced law in that city until 1938, and her sister Sidonia who lived out her adult life in Romania. Sidi became known, in my father's parlance, as "my aunt in Romania."

Among the numerous Buchsbaums, a few smart or lucky ones managed to emigrate before the war.

Sidonia, Clara, and Norbert Babad

Ostrava, Czechoslovakia

Clara Babad

My great-grandfather, Sigmund Babad, descended from a line of distinguished rabbis that dates from the Middle Ages. He managed a large liqueur factory but his income didn't meet his family's needs. They lived in Bielitz in Silesia, an Austrian province before 1918. The town, located in southern Poland today, straddled the corner where German, Czech, and Polish borders met. When a private bank in nearby Ostrava offered

Sigmund an excellent job, he rejected it. He believed his employer would, as promised, make him a partner in the liqueur factory.

When his elder daughter Sidonia became engaged, he obtained a loan from relatives using his wife's beautiful jewelry collection as security. He settled for funds far less than the jewelry's value, maintaining a pattern of unfortunate financial decisions.

Sigmund died prematurely of pneumonia a month before his daughter Clara's marriage to my grandfather. His employer did not honor any of his promises: he did not provide a dowry for Clara, nor a university education for her brother Norbert or financial support for Sigmund's wife, Jeanette Reitmann.

Jeanette, born into a prominent Austrian family, spoke French at home instead of German—a common practice among the Austrian upper classes, according to my father.

Her grandfather had been the royal coachmaker for the Austrian Imperial Court and also supplied coaches and sleighs to the Imperial Court of Russia. Her family was quite wealthy and accepted in Viennese society.

Family history does not speculate on how Sigmund managed to captivate such a wealthy, socially prominent woman. Perhaps his lineage of distinguished rabbis made him an eligible match.

Jeanette's brother, Rudolph Reitmann, became a physician and entered the Austrian Imperial Army, reaching the rank of major general by the time he retired in 1918. Before World War I he was personal physician to Archduchess Zitta of Bourbon-Parma, the wife of Archduke Charles of Habsburg, the later emperor and empress of Austria (1916-1918). Rudolph delivered some of their royal offspring.

Ignatz Buchsbaum

My grandfather Ignatz Buchsbaum, one of six children, grew up in Krzeszowice, some twenty miles east of Ostrava, with the pungency of freshly milled wood. His father, Moric (Morris), owned a lumber business. After Ignatz survived a diphtheria outbreak that took the life of his older brother, his mother, Fanny, cruelly rejected him. "Why did he have to die while you survived?" she allegedly said to Ignatz, instilling in him an enduring sense of inferiority.

In his family history my father wrote this of Ignatz: "My father grew up as an unloved child, starved for approval and acceptance. He also seemed to be sad. At least he looked sad in all the childhood pictures I ever saw."

His mother's hatred for Ignatz, who had lost his hearing in one ear from the diphtheria, later extended to my grandmother, my father, and his sister, Gretl. While other granddaughters received valuable jewelry when they turned eighteen, Gretl was given a modest gold bracelet.

Ignatz grew up to be shy, introverted, and often suspicious of others' intentions. After he graduated from high school, he was apprenticed to a lumber merchant to prepare him for eventually taking over his father's business. Denied the university education he yearned for, Ignatz secretly left the lumber business and, for three years, apprenticed with booksellers in the nearby German city of Breslau where he had served his apprenticeship in the lumber business. His first job, in a bookstore in Vienna, was followed by a year in a bookstore in Prague, specializing in university texts and scholarly works. In 1901 he opened his own bookstore on the main square in Přívoz, then a community adjacent to Ostrava.

Two features marked out Přívoz as a desirable venue for a bookstore. As a major railroad junction and a market town, Přívoz witnessed a flow of people and, overall, a population increase. My grandfather's bookshop profited from all the activity.

A love story

In 1904 my grandfather Ignatz and my grandmother Clara met in the city of Bielitz, near the ever-changing border between Czechoslovakia and present-day Poland. The story of their old-world courtship and marriage carried elements of the fairy tales I loved to read as a child. I'm sure my father contributed to the feeling. He frequently began stories about his family with "When I was a little boy..." Even the name Czechoslovakia sounded far away and make-believe.

In the Buchsbaum family history my father wrote in the 1970s, he described his mother as "a beautiful, young heiress." Clara was certainly very pretty but, due to her father's financial mismanagement, hardly an heiress. The engaging Clara and the poor but handsome book lover Ignatz met by chance at the finishing school my grandmother attended. They fell in love. My father described it as a "lovely, sweet courtship, a bit on the shy side." He wrote:

My father traveled to the engagement party that was held in Bielitz by train, the only means of travel then, during a blizzard. Because of the storm, the train was delayed for many hours and my father arrived in Bielitz in the middle of the night.

The streetcars were not running anymore, there were no cabs at the station (only horse cabs at that time, of course), and my father couldn't walk the couple of miles through the deep snow. How did he manage? Well, my mother told me that he arrived, soaked and half

*frozen, sitting next to the driver on top of a milk wagon in the dawn's
early light. Still, what impressed my mother most was his new
beautiful grey suit with a stunning and very chic red and yellow
embroidered vest.*

Two events shadowed their wedding: the illness and subsequent
death of Clara's father, who made the couple promise not to
delay the nuptials, and the Babad family's dire financial straits.

Clara and Ignatz married on February 7, 1905 and moved into an
apartment across the street from Ignatz's bookstore in Přívoz.
Their first child, my Aunt Gretl, was born on February 9, 1907. In
1910 the family moved into a new building at 173 Bahnhofstrasse
(Station Street) across the street from a stately square just in
time for the birth of my father, Hans, on Christmas Eve.

173 Nádražní (formerly Bahnhofstrasse)

The bookstore—and eventually the publishing company—
occupied the ground floor and part of the second floor. The
family lived on both floors in a very large apartment that
included servants' quarters.

This postcard was printed by I. Buchsbaum publishers

My father wrote of his mother:

She was indeed amazing. She took fine care of her family while working full time in the business and taking care of the house. Of course, we had servants, quite a number of them, but I still remember my mother going marketing every morning to the farmers' market, hustling back and forth between office and apartment, taking care of us when we were sick, meeting us when we returned from school, even helping me take care of my assorted animals.

Though Clara enfolded her family in a protective, loving embrace, she also was adamant about matters of class and breeding. When her cherished brother Norbert, a lawyer educated at the University of Vienna, married Annie, a non-Jewish, twice-divorced woman not up to Clara's standards, my grandmother expressed contempt. She was certain Annie had trapped Norbert in a ploy as old as civilization.

Eventually Clara attained a bookseller's license, which made her a full partner in I. Buchsbaum, a major publisher of 'varia,' meaning books that didn't fit into any specific category. They were published in German and Czech.

The inventory included various trade books for carpenters, metal workers, and others in the building trades. Self-improvement books on etiquette, correspondence, and the easy study of foreign languages were innovative in their day.

The company even published the Czech edition of *The Perfect Marriage* by the Belgian physician, Van der Velde, the most famous book on sex in marriage for the pre-World War II German speaking readership.

I. Buchsbaum also produced periodicals, including a monthly magazine on popular science, another on nature studies, and a series of weeklies for the study of foreign languages. All found places on the company's shelves and in its rapidly expanding mail-order catalogue.

Ignatz was featured in an exhibit of prominent businessmen from pre-war Ostrava. (The exhibition was held in 2012 in Ostrava, CR)

Spinning with ideas, Ignatz demonstrated an ability to anticipate and capitalize on what would prove popular, and thus lucrative. His firm also offered children's educational toys and games. My grandfather even introduced the Biro ballpoint pen to Czechoslovakia.

Mai 1925

Ignatz Buchsbaum, author's grandfather

When the Czech government established public libraries countrywide, my grandfather filled their shelves by buying up other publishers' overstock and books at estate sales. In the meantime, his business grew rapidly and exponentially. The tremendous success of I. Buchsbaum publishing reflected Ostrava's growth. Despite an economic decline after the Armistice in 1918, my grandfather continued to identify and anticipate what people wanted and needed before they realized it themselves.

Much to his shame, Ignatz never learned to drive and learned only a smattering of Hebrew. When he attended services at his synagogue, he instructed the chauffeur to drop him off several blocks from the entrance. He was a modest man who shunned

13

pretense. In Temple, he dreaded being called to the *bimah* to recite a prayer or read from the *Torah*.

When World War I ended, the city grew, gradually incorporating surrounding towns and districts. It absorbed Přívoz, a market town, and Vítkovice, the famous steel-producing center. A burgeoning citizenry created a market for businesses. With the rise of a solid middle class came painters, writers, musicians, and theatre companies that provided culture.

Both the general and Jewish populations increased. By 1938 Ostrava boasted eight synagogues for the seven to eight thousand Jewish people residing there—out of a total population of almost two hundred fifty thousand. At that time, the population of Czechoslovakia was about ten million.

Map of Czechoslovakia

At home Gretl and Hans had a governess who taught them until they were about ten years old and entered public schools. After her high school graduation, Gretl went to a finishing school, a special type of education for wealthy girls expected to manage households and entertain for the ambitious, successful men they were to marry.

The years between Gretl's birth in 1907 and my father's in 1910 until the German invasion of Czechoslovakia in March 1939 were prosperous and mostly happy for the family. My father was clearly his mother's joy, a golden son whose every utterance and activity delighted her. Early on, my father was consumed by an interest in the natural world, assembling a collection of lizards and other amphibians in a terrarium he constructed himself.

Later his interest turned to chemistry. Ignatz set up a small laboratory in my father's bedroom. Inevitably, there was an explosion but that didn't prevent my grandfather from developing a line of chemistry kits for older children, called "The Little Chemist."

Hans and his lion c. 1912

One theme that emerges is my father's yearning for a more omnipresent father. Ignatz was engaged with his children in their younger years, laughing, joking, reading to them, and playing games. When my father sang "Oh My Little Bear" as he rocked me, he was passing down an expression of tenderness from his own father.

As time went on, Ignatz became increasingly aloof and preoccupied with his publishing company. My father complained that "Mr. Latzin [a school friend's father] always plays with us and shows us chemical experiments," to which Ignatz answered, "Mr. Latzin has a job and gets paid regularly and doesn't have to worry after work, while I have to build something for you and think about it all the time."

My father recalled a later incident, however, when he was in high school, that demonstrated his father's deep empathy and protective instinct. He wrote in his family history:

My father noted one evening that I seemed depressed. I told him that I was scared because a big, strong kid, two grades ahead of me, had threatened to beat me up when I came to school the next day. When I came out of the classroom for lunch, who was standing in front of the door but my father, carrying a heavy cane, waiting for me, so he could protect me against the bully. I can still remember the feeling of being loved and secure that suddenly seemed to envelop me that day.

Clara's devotion was absolute. Her protectiveness made her a lioness. One day when she returned from shopping, she noticed one of my father's ears was red and asked what had happened.

"I was naughty and Miss pulled my ear," he explained. My grandmother immediately fired the nursemaid.

On Sundays the family took the train into the countryside for walks and afternoon coffee, or they visited my grandfather's relatives in Krzeszowice.

Ignatz and Clara Buchsbaum

It must have seemed as though the universe delivered fairy dust to the Buchsbaums. Being born so early in the twentieth century, I imagined my father carried in his cells the romance of the nineteenth-century Austrian-Hungarian Empire. Later, when we traveled in central Europe, he always knew which hotel or coffeehouse to patronize. In Vienna it was the Central or perhaps the Mozart Café, part of the Hotel Sacher, which served their famous Sachertorte. In Berlin, the Hotel Kempinski was *de rigueur* and, of course, Kranzler's for afternoon coffee. Pastry was practically required.

Jewish residents of Moravia mostly spoke German. My grandparents, however, ensured that their children attended both German and Czech schools so that they became bilingual.

The bond between my father and his mother, probably forged at his birth, was inviolate and endured until Clara's death. My father reiterated frequently how his mother had loved and supported him, and how he, probably spoiled by the cascade of her affection and approval, became a lazy, rebellious teenager who ignored his studies. He preferred competitive skiing and track events under the umbrella of the Maccabi Olympics, a Jewish sports organization.

My father failed Greek in high school, necessitating the hiring of a tutor so he could obtain the *Abitur*, a diploma needed for entrance into university. When he settled into his student rooms near Charles University in Prague, he studied for a law degree just like his Uncle Norbert. Norbert was a mannered, effete law school graduate though he always regretted not going to medical school. My grandfather pressured my father into studying law, insisting it would prepare him for taking over the publishing house.

John Buchsbaum

Eventually, my father grew up. At Charles University, for the first time ever, he experienced antisemitism and fought a duel with sabers because of an antisemitic remark. He carried a scar on the back of his head but assured me he'd won. During his university years he joined a Zionist fraternity, where he developed lifelong friendships.

Applying himself to his studies, my father graduated with a Doctor of Jurisprudence degree. Ignatz was so proud that he bought my father a sports car as a graduation gift. My father then completed compulsory military service as a cavalry officer in the Czech army from 1934-1936. He joined the family publishing company afterwards.

Then the unspeakable happened.

On August 27, 1937, without any warning, Ignatz committed suicide by hanging. While he had experienced episodes of depression, his suicide shocked and saddened the family and the community. His obituary noted that he carried in his pocket a receipt for a new, custom-made tennis outfit. This sudden, tragic event was heartbreaking.

When I was about ten years old, I asked my father about the cause of my grandfather's death. He paused. "He had a tooth infection that went into his whole body," he said. To my knowledge that was the only time my father lied to me. I'm grateful he did although I was shocked to learn the truth from my mother after my father died.

After Ignatz's suicide my father and grandmother ran the publishing company, continuing as before. My father wrote that he experienced his own limitations. He saw himself as a competent administrator but realized he lacked his father's imagination, which had elevated the publishing enterprise to a name brand in Czechoslovakia.

2 INVASION (1939)

Ostrava, Czechoslovakia

In retrospect it seems most members of the greater Buchsbaum family did not recognize the ominous rise of Nazi-Germany. While friends and a few relatives emigrated to countries beyond continental Europe—the United States, England, South Africa, Palestine—my family did not act to get out until it was too late.

Sometime before he died in 1937, my usually pessimistic grandfather expressed his fear that the Nazis would take over Czechoslovakia and the family would have to flee for their lives. My father tried to convince him that was impossible since Nazism appealed only to Germans, not Czechs. Furthermore, my father countered, any German attempt to interfere with Czechoslovakia would activate the Czech army.

Was my grandfather, seemingly prescient in publishing, also able to anticipate probable events for Czechoslovakia? Others certainly did and got out. Perhaps they recognized how, in the late 1930s, the predominance of German-speaking Czech citizens in Bohemia and Moravia would provide Hitler with justification to invade and annex the area and claim it as the German Sudetenland. Hitler maintained that non-Jewish, German-speaking citizens were "ethnic Germans," which many have disputed.

In March 1938 the Germans annexed Austria. Uncle Norbert, who had been living in Vienna with his wife Annie, crossed the border illegally at night and joined the Buchsbaum family household in Ostrava. Of course, Clara provided a home for her cherished brother, despite the unwelcome arrival of his wife. Norbert's presence also produced tension. "He inserted himself into every business or private situation, offering opinions and making a nuisance of himself," my father wrote.

Meanwhile, the situation in Czechoslovakia began to heat up. In October 1938 thousands of Jews besieged foreign consulates, desperately seeking a haven. They found the doors closed. The quotas in the United States, for example, allotted twenty-five hundred visas per year to applicants from Czechoslovakia.

The German army invaded Ostrava on the evening of March 14, 1939. My father was recalled to active army duty. German tanks crossed the border, overpowering the opposition of the Czech forces. France did not honor its alliance with Czechoslovakia and Great Britain followed suit.

The invasion marked the abrupt end of the Buchsbaums' privileged life and the start of a five-year endeavor to survive. Until I read my father's family history, I carried romantic fantasies of pre-war life that combined elements of nineteenth-century operettas and films such as the original *Grand Hotel*. I pictured my father in a scarlet-sashed uniform waltzing at balls in Prague and Vienna where elegant women in satin evening dress and furs acquiesced to stolen kisses behind potted palms. It was in that world I imagined myself, a world that probably ended with the World War I Armistice when my father was just eight years old.

The 1939 invasion ultimately led to the extermination of approximately 263,000 Czech Jews. Eighty thousand of them were from the provinces of Bohemia and Moravia.

Why hadn't my father, a sophisticated intellectual and publisher, heeded the same warning signals that prompted others to leave the country? It pains me to think critically of the father I have always worshipped, but I believe his own arrogance may have blinded him to the family's vulnerability. They were prominent members of the Ostrava Jewish community and the general business community. Did he think wealth and social position would protect them? Possibly. I can imagine his sneering at the very idea of Hitler, a lower-class failure, a housepainter without education or breeding. It would have been unimaginable to my father to fear such a man.

In addition, the treaty with France and an assumed agreement with Great Britain may have provided a false sense of security. Many Czechs felt they'd been "sold out" by those countries, which failed to defend Czechoslovakia. Their failure reflected a 1939 mentality of preserving peace regardless of the ultimate cost.

Desperately trying to obtain visas for himself and his mother, my father went from embassy to embassy, seeking entrée into England, Switzerland, Cuba, or any South American country. The doors seemed closed everywhere. For this central European family, the idea of emigrating to South America involved a leap of imagination but it also reflected their fundamental confidence in their ability to navigate the future. They studied Spanish as they awaited their visas.

After the invasion, the iron fist of Nazi occupation gripped the country. On the day of the invasion my father was in London on business, desperately attempting to transfer funds into an English bank. When he flew back to Prague, he was stunned by the SS presence in the airport. And still the family thought there was time. They shipped furniture, paintings, and china to Rotterdam, Holland, placing their possessions in storage to furnish their future lives.

Shortly after the invasion by German troops four men appeared in the office identifying themselves as members of the Gestapo. The family was forbidden to enter the place of business. Shortly thereafter, a new director, Mr. Erwin Hruschka, a former employee of the company, was installed.[1]

The family was forbidden to withdraw any assets related to the company. One bonus was the retention of the firm's loyal secretary who entered into a romantic relationship with one of the members of the Gestapo. Her boyfriend became helpful for a price, namely my father's convertible sportscar. This heinous connection saved my father's life.

My father was finally able to get a temporary visa for England since a fraternity brother who had succeeded in getting there put up financial guarantees for him. "This is why I could save myself, while the rest of my family perished," he wrote. He never stopped working to get my grandmother Clara, his sister Gretl, her husband Hugo, and their daughter Susi out of Europe but he never wrote anything more about them in his family history.

Perhaps grief, guilt or a combination of the two kept him from writing of their ultimate loss.

In my own quest to know my family more deeply, understandings emerge, sometimes gradually, other times like a geyser. I now realize my father's self-aggrandizing habit of claiming to always make the right decision was an elaborate defense. He criticized colleagues and friends for poor judgement and bad decisions when he may have failed when it mattered most in his life.

My father described this time as "terror-filled days and nights, always looking over your shoulder, afraid to linger on the street and talk to friends, fearful of going to the one café Jews were allowed to patronize."

My father had surrendered his passport and Clara's to the Gestapo in order to obtain exit permits so they could leave Czechoslovakia. To retrieve them he drove to Gestapo headquarters and parked in front of the building. My father wrote in his book:

Nobody who has not lived through our experience can imagine the terror under which Jews existed at that time. You stayed home as much as you could and went to bed each night dreading the knock on the door that could come in the early morning hours. If you absolutely had to go out and happened to meet an acquaintance and stopped to talk, you constantly looked over your shoulder to see whether anyone was listening in. For entertainment, you could only listen to the radio because all public places, theatres, movies, were off-limits for Jews.

And I had to go to Gestapo headquarters. You might understand what it meant for a Jew to walk into the lion's den. Today, more than forty years later, I still have nightmares about it.

Five or six men and women were lined up facing the wall with their toes touching the baseboard. I was asked my name and the purpose of the visit, and then had to join the others, lined up against the wall. I was scared stiff.

One after the other, my companions in agony were called away, and it was my turn. I was taken to an office and told to stand near the door, while a man sat behind a desk across the room. He looked at me in silence for a while and my spirit reached bottom, and then he asked whether I remembered him. I said that I didn't. "My name is so and so and we went to grade school together."

Well, I still didn't remember him. Then he asked me what I wanted, and when I told him, he opened his desk drawer, took out two passports, and threw them toward me, and they came skidding across the floor almost to my feet. I picked them up, thanked him, and left.

I had gotten my passport, and I had been treated better than a Jew could expect to be treated by the Gestapo. I walked down the stairs with a wonderful light feeling of relief. As I walked out the front door, a soldier in the black uniform of the SS hailed me and asked, "You Buchsbaum?" I said yes—and he grabbed my arm and dragged me back into the building. He opened an office door and called out: "I got him!"

Like lightning it hit me: That's the end. And then, another man, in civilian clothes, stuck out his head: "Did you get the passports?" It was my secretary's boyfriend. I walked down to my car on shaky knees and weak legs.

There was a "bonus" at the conclusion of this terrifying episode. Once the Germans took over, all identity documents for Jews, including passports, were stamped with a big red "J" for Jew on the first page to identify the bearer and mark him for appropriate treatment. When we examined our passports, we found to our amazement that my former schoolmate had failed to stamp the "J" on them, obviously an intentional favor.

---

1. Information supplied by John Buchsbaum in an affidavit obtained in September 1957 as part of the process of applying to the German government for reparations.

3   ESCAPE (1939-1941)

Ostrava, Czechoslovakia

On June 19, 1939 the Buchsbaum telephone rang and a man's voice said, "You have to leave today. Do not be in this city tomorrow. You will be arrested in the morning." My father recognized the voice of an acquaintance in the Ostrauer police who must have known about the impending arrest and took the risk of warning my father. He quickly packed two suitcases and drove to his sister's house to say goodbye. Hugging him, she said tearfully, "We'll never see each other again." Her pessimism surprised my father.

I picture his last embrace with his mother. She would have held onto him even as she pushed him out the door. He left with his father's gold pocket watch and his mother's gold bracelet sewn into his coat lining. All his life my father was impatient at long goodbyes, perhaps because of those final minutes with his mother.

Did she pack him goose liver pâté sandwiches, precisely wrapped? An apple? A piece of strudel? His memoir doesn't say. But he did write that he watched the familiar landscape of his birthplace disappear as the train slid out of the station. He sensed he would never see it again.

I arrived in Prague that evening and went to the hotel my father and I had always stayed in. As I entered the lobby, I saw a number of SS characters lounging in big chairs, talking bombastically. Once again, I had inadvertently walked into the lion's den: the hotel was the transient residence for the SS members in Prague. As I walked up to the desk, an SS man called arrogantly from his seat to the desk clerk: "Get me a first-class plane ticket to Berlin for tomorrow morning." Looking at him, I decided that he had been a grocery clerk before joining the SS.

If you discover a trace of arrogance in that last statement, you are right. Though the Nazis might have considered me sub-human as a Jew, I still felt that I was a member of the elite, the Jewish aristocracy.

The following morning, I tried to reach the British Consulate by phone to find out whether my visa had arrived, but the number was perpetually busy. Then I walked over the few blocks to see whether I could go in and ask the question in person, but the line of people trying to get in stretched around the block and I knew it would take hours, if I could get in at all. The answer to the question of how to reach them struck me.

People might ignore telephone calls or letters, but nobody ignores a telegram, especially if it comes with answer prepaid. I went to the nearest post office (telegrams in Europe are the responsibility of the post office) and sent a telegram, reply prepaid, asking about the visa.

When I returned to my hotel after dinner that night, I found the reply informing me that the visa had indeed arrived and inviting me for an interview at the consulate.

The next morning, I had no problem walking in ahead of all those who were waiting in line because of the telegram inviting me to come. Within ten minutes I had an English visa stamped into my passport.

There still remained the question of getting to England safely. We knew that immediately following the German occupation of Czechoslovakia, literally thousands of wealthy Jews had just packed up to get to England by train. In those early days you didn't need a visa because an agreement between Czechoslovakia and Great Britain provided entry on passport without visa, and the British conscientiously honored this agreement until the law was changed a few days after.

Over the years I'd read my father's story in full at least five times before that amazing last paragraph penetrated. I was breathless. Friends of theirs simply boarded a train and got out? There were a precious three days to go, if you were willing to leave—leave your car, your money, your publishing company, your status, and your privileged life. They might have gotten out. Clara, Gretl, Hugo, and my cousin Susi could have survived by getting on a train and traveling to ports in France or Holland where an overnight boat train transported travelers across the English Channel to England. To safety. To life.

Facing my father's indecisiveness is very difficult. Other dimensions and layers lie beneath my father's suspenseful tale of escape. In his writing he reveals himself at age twenty-nine not as the hero I worshipped throughout my childhood and beyond, but as a mere mortal capable of a mistake in judgement. But such a mistake!

I idolized my father until the end of his life and I idealized him as well. I always trusted him totally. But the loss of his family angered me at those times when I yearned for the comfort and companionship of Clara and Susi.

Had my father been uninformed about Hitler's intentions as set forth in his book *Mein Kampf*? While the 'Final Solution,' the systematic extermination of the Jews, had yet to be formulated, some friends and a few family members had made the decision to leave a few years earlier. Once Czechoslovakia was invaded, the sense of urgency increased but my family still delayed.

I know there was great concern about getting money out of the country. Money is a theme that pervades this account of my family. It fills my grandmother's letters. But my father, his sister Gretl, and her husband Hugo were young. Given their educations, they could have felt confident about starting new lives. Perhaps it was not in their characters to break the rules. If the law threatened death for taking money abroad, they couldn't or wouldn't have risked trying.

Is it fair to criticize my father for actions he didn't take? To condemn his brother-in-law Hugo for dallying? My father told me that Hugo, an arrogant and self-important engineer-manager in the city's Vítkovice Iron Works, believed he could make a deal with the Germans. Why, oh why, didn't they all leave during those precious three days? Perhaps they hadn't yet obtained their exit visas from the Gestapo. If so, to have left would have constituted additional risk.

I don't understand all the particulars and there is no one to ask. The mature part of me knows my challenge is to accept my father's judgment eighty years after he made those decisions—to accept without censure what cannot be changed. When I was young, I looked up to my father as all-knowing, godlike. My need for security required that. Now, however, my love can be more realistic and, therefore, more forgiving. I choose to believe he did his very best to protect the family he loved more than anything.

Even with an exit visa from the Gestapo, my father's perilous journey to freedom was far from assured. To travel through Germany and get to the Channel coast, the gateway to England, demanded careful planning and nerves of steel.

We had heard of the indignities and harassment to which Jews in the early exodus were exposed when they crossed the border in first-class compartments on express trains. At the borders, Jews had to get off the train with their luggage to have it inspected, and this consisted of having the contents of suitcases thrown out on the platform, having to undress for body searches, all this accompanied by insults and curses. If the train took off in the meantime, some of the people remained behind and had to wait there for the next day's train. I wanted to avoid this, and I also feared that the people at the border might have been informed that I narrowly escaped arrest in Ostrava and might have a list on which my name was placed and would arrest me.

I went to the Czech travel office to find a safer way. I was wearing the pin of the Czechoslovak Officers' Association and I saw behind the counter a clerk wearing a similar pin. I turned to him and asked for a schedule of trains to London. He said, without looking up, "Take the 9 p.m. express directly to the Hook of Holland."

I pointed to my pin. "Brother, I want to go a safer way."

His gaze met mine and he understood immediately, and told me to sit down and wait. After a while, he called me back to the counter, handed me a slip filled with data, and explained the complicated schedule.

To avoid border control officers, the route required taking a series of early morning local milk trains for border crossings. The itinerary also included one change of train in Berlin, the command center of Nazi-Germany.

My father followed the schedule exactly and arrived in Holland without mishap but extremely hungry. The law prohibited carrying more than ten marks, equivalent to one dollar, out of the country. A kind and perceptive gentleman invited my father for lunch in the dining car. My father wrote, "I have loved the Dutch ever since."

Following a trip across the English channel, my father arrived safely in London on June 23, 1939. He was met by Irwin and Gerta Katona, close friends who had managed to get to England before him.

During his university years my father had had a love affair with the older, beautiful, and married Gerta. Perhaps among a sophisticated, urban strata in the pre-war years, the relationship was simply part of a young man's education, a way to gain worldly experience. I mention this because my father was old-fashioned and moralistic about just this kind of behavior.

Most notable, though, was the friendship between my father, Irwin, and Gerta, which sustained them during the Blitz and endured until Irwin and Gerta died decades later. During the Blitz in London, when the Germans sent bombers across the English Channel every night, the Katonas offered my father emotional and perhaps some financial support. They frequently invited him to dinner, knowing without his explanations that he could not always afford to eat.

After the war, when Britain suffered many shortages, my parents sent the Katonas care packages with coffee, sugar, nylon stockings, and other items simply not available or strictly rationed. I met them in 1960 when my mother and I spent a week in London. There was clear evidence of fondness between my mother and this gracious couple who embraced her warmly. Gerta held my mother's hand as we toured the sights of London together.

My father's admission to England on a temporary visa was predicated on his emigrating elsewhere as soon as possible. He certainly was not allowed to work. He lived temporarily in Torquay, an English seaside resort in Devonshire. There he met some Quaker ladies who wanted to study German. He taught a weekly class and acquired some individual students. Both endeavors helped marginally with his finances and endeared the English people to him for the rest of his life.

The handful of permanent Jewish residents in Torquay, along with some Jewish retirees living in hotels and boardinghouses, hired a hotel hall and engaged a rabbi to conduct High Holiday services. My father wrote poignantly of this time:

I have never been a pious Jew, but had always attended services at the High Holidays, and now, as a refugee because of my religion, it was even more important to me than before. So I went to attend services on Rosh Hashanah. Being away from home in a foreign country as a refugee, still hearing the same songs and prayers I had always listened to with my family in the past, made me sad and I started to cry.

After the service, a very pretty, well-dressed lady talked to me, asking me who I was and where I had come from. She introduced herself as Mrs. Lees, the wife of a local physician, and invited me to dinner.

In her warm and gracious family my father found acceptance and was given opportunities to socialize with educated and sympathetic English people.

Knowing his law degree was useless outside Czechoslovakia, my father learned the leather-cutting trade, which enhanced his chances for admission to the United States. He searched for an opportunity to ply his new skill and soon discovered one in nearby Newton Abbot, a town with a leather factory that paid its apprentices a small salary. The young factory owner was extremely kind. He taught my father the rudiments of leather cutting and introduced him to golf, even giving him a set of used clubs. Sometimes the two young men would take off in the boss's sporty Jaguar for a round of the game.

During that time my father received a letter from his mother, sent from Italy to the Katonas, who forwarded it from London. Clara had managed to leave Czechoslovakia under a special program to promote Italian tourism. My father obtained friends' financial guarantees to bring his mother to England, but the fall of France in June 1940 dashed those plans. The Italians joined the war on the side of Germany that very month, changing Clara's status to that of an interned person. This meant that she could not travel within Italy without permission. My father experienced the fall of France as a personal, terrible trauma.

I believed that the war was lost, and that the Germans would control all of Europe. Being continental and being excitable, I told that to my cockney foreman. He had the right answer, though I didn't know it then. He put his hand on my shoulder and said: "Don't get excited, laddie, we still have our navy (rhymes with 'ivy')."

After the German Blitzkrieg that overran Denmark, Norway, Holland, and Belgium, and the subsequent capitulation of France, my father's thinking changed. He'd been waiting out the war, hoping to emigrate to America, when the British government decreed resident aliens could join the British Army and help fight the Germans. My father traveled to the recruiting station in Exeter and filled out the required forms to enlist.

I had made it clear on the form that I was an officer of an allied nation (Czechoslovakia) and thought I would be greeted by the colonel as a fellow officer. No such luck. He was one of the World War I relics, the type described by British cartoonists as 'Colonel Blimp.' He slowly read through my forms, while he kept me standing in front of his desk. I decided to ask him something that was very much on my mind. I knew that whatever happened in the end, Czechoslovakia would never be the same again and I would not care to go back. So, I said, "Colonel, if I join the British Army, will I get British citizenship when the war is over?" He looked at me for a moment and said, "Why should we give you citizenship? We are fighting this war so that people like you can go back where you came from."

As my father expected, he was turned down. This rejection ignited an impulse to get to the United States at all costs and fight for America, which would surely enter the war. He moved back to London just in time for the nightly bombing raids of the Battle of Britain. My father frequently described the hours spent in bomb shelters and the Underground, the London metro system, extolling the spirit of the British, their "boundless courage and determination" under extremely difficult and terrifying conditions.

In December 1940 my father's turn came. He received a visa to the United States. The challenge was transportation across the Atlantic Ocean where submarines were legion. Luck of every kind prevailed. Two months later my father landed in Halifax, Nova Scotia, and took a train to Penn Station in New York City where the young adult sons of his cousin Benjamin Buchsbaum picked him up. The journey was nothing short of a miracle for my refugee father. Now he could begin the rest of his life.

4 SEPARATION (1939-1944)

Florence and San Donato Val di Comino

Clara remained in Ostrava and helped to run the family's publishing company from June through August 1939. She used her expertise in the business, including marketing strategies for new books, and seemed reconciled to losing ownership and sharing management with a Nazi-appointed publisher—a former employee.

Her June 16, 1939 letter to my father in London closed with motherly advice:

Now my dear Hannesl, I still must tell you, think of yourself, be egoistic and use your elbows. Stay healthy, my darling, eat well and much, and be happy inside. Maybe you can still sign up for an English language course. I kiss you from the depth of my heart, also your dear friends, greet them from me with much gratitude.

Always with much love, Mutti

By September 27, 1939, Clara settled in Florence, Italy, at the Pensione Balestri, situated on a lovely square one block from the Ponte Vecchio, the famous bridge across the River Arno.

Pensione Balestri, Piazza Mentana 5, Florence, Italy

Under a special program the German government had established, she transferred some money from an Ostrava bank for an extended vacation. Her letters contained veiled references to the frequent harassment by the Gestapo and SS in Ostrava. They were searching for my father, who had evaded arrest. She felt insecure in that atmosphere. Clearly, she had self-censored her correspondence.

Since Italy had not yet entered the war, Clara could send letters to England, and did that at least twice a week.

On September 27, 1939, she wrote:

My dear (above everything) beloved Hannesl!

Yesterday I received your belated letter from 9/4 with outdated news, since I had already received your two following letters. Nevertheless, I felt great joy to read your dear and good words for me. It is most beautiful here; the heat has subsided, and it is very comfortable and sunny. I hope to continue to have a restful time. I thought about moving here for good, because it will be so much cheaper here in the fall, but I fear that the evenings will be too lonely for me.

Your loving you always, Mutti

A following letter offers details about financial issues and social invitations. Deciding to be frugal, Clara did not accompany some old friends and newer acquaintances on a Mediterranean excursion. The tone of the letter carries recognition that her circumstances had changed and perhaps some subtle regret.

One of the mysteries and marvels of the early war years was how correspondence flowed from Ostrava and Italy to my father in England and, until 1941, to him and other Buchsbaums in the United States. The International Red Cross made communication possible by 'Red Cross Letters,' brief messages of no more than twenty-five words that could be sent once a month. But my grandmother's letters to my father were written on two sides of thin tissue writing paper in beautiful penmanship. They combined expressions of deepest love with practical advice, taking far more than twenty-five words. The letters also meticulously documented her efforts to obtain a visa and demonstrated her tenacity, fortitude, and resourcefulness in her quest to leave Europe.

She wrote on January 9, 1940:

My one and only beloved Hannesl!

I am starting again with letter #1 and am confirming your dear letter #22 from January 1, as well as the previous one from your trip. First, many dear thanks, my darling, for your efforts on my behalf, it makes me happy to know that someone is thinking of me with care and worries, and when I am sometimes seized with a deep sorrow, it is only the thought of you, my dearest Hannesl, that gives me the strength to bear life, and also the worry about Gretl, whom I would love to know is safe. You are trying so hard that I can join you, and I will do everything to obtain an extension for my stay here until I can come to you.

Clara's letters throughout 1940 and 1941 recount the details of her efforts to obtain visas for anywhere outside Europe. Always, yesterday's possibilities evaporated today. Palestine, Bolivia, Peru, Chile, Brazil, Shanghai, once possible destinations, were either deemed too remote for Clara or were no longer issuing visas. Consulates were besieged and even closed without notice. Affidavits had to be obtained and guarantees provided, but then paperwork expired and the whole process began again. Rumors sent hope spinning upwards, only to dissolve as another door closed.

Ben Buchsbaum continued working tirelessly on my grandmother's behalf, contributing to her support in Italy and sending the funds that accompanied visa applications. While he ultimately brought twenty-eight refugees to the United States, including my father, sponsoring and launching some of them into new businesses in America, my grandmother was tethered in Europe. It seemed no amount of money or labor could carry her to freedom.

Somehow, Clara studied English, Italian, and Spanish, wrote letters to friends and family still in Czechoslovakia and in other countries, and wrote to my father. She wrote that the Pensione was to be renovated and she planned to join the owners and other residents at their mountain retreat.

My grandmother was amazingly resourceful. Her letters reflect every possible effort to reach freedom. She remained undaunted, sending telegrams, filling out forms, consulting other refugees, visiting travel agents and consulates in Rome, and following every lead. Throughout, she maintained psychological stability and a positive attitude. Hope and confidence drove her efforts. Her letters reflect both.

In November 1940, a month before my father's birthday, she wrote:

My above everything beloved!

I am sending you my deepest warmest wishes for your birthday. It is your 30th, is it possible at all, I can hardly believe it! I still see my little one with the curls in front of me. My above everything beloved child, may the dear God always keep you healthy and protect you from any suffering [harm] and give you much happiness and joy, my good-hearted child, for you deserve it. May it be easy for you to build for yourself a joyful, happy and secure future and to get to our dear good cousin. I am so happy when I receive a letter from you. I am always, and will be on your birthday, with you. With all my thoughts and deepest wishes, I bless you from my deepest heart, you my good, beloved child. I am longing for you and hope firmly for a happy reunion. Many deepest wishes and kisses also from Gretl, Hugo and Susi, they are always asking about you and love you very much. I embrace you again, my everything, with the warmest wishes, and a happy beginning for your new year of life and kiss you in love and closeness.

Your Mutti

Clara carried on a voluminous correspondence with relatives, friends, consulates, and immigration authorities, too. She describes the roadblocks, but never complains about them. She worries constantly about Gretl and her family, still in Czechoslovakia, and mentions, like all good grandmothers, that

Gretl's daughter Susi is an outstanding math student and has won some math competitions.

I wondered how those evenings really were for her, those moments when she was alone with no activity to distract her from worry. Her own future and that of Gretl, Hugo, and Susi must have weighed heavily on her heart. While she occasionally refers to them and her worry for them, she mostly recounts their everyday lives and efforts to obtain visas. How much did Clara and her family know at the end of 1940 about the Nazi treatment of Jews? Probably very little. She prays for her family's reunion and doesn't express fears for their ultimate survival. Sometimes she invokes the help of "the good God," but if she ever contemplates her own death and that of the family, she doesn't express it.

Certain relatives, particularly her brother Norbert's wife, Annie, earn her scorn. My father commented in his memoir that his mother had firm and immutable ideas about their social class and her refined upbringing. Clara reiterates in her letters the scandal of her brother Norbert's marriage. Clara not only rejected association with Annie but pressured my father, Gretl, and other relatives to follow her lead.

I wonder if maintaining her social standards helped Clara defend against corrosive anxiety about the well-being of Gretl and Susi. Amid the privations, the cold, limited funds, and limitless needs, perhaps she could distract and reassure herself with petty observations. To avoid confronting her worst fears, she seemed to obsess somewhat about matters of class and refinement—and their absence in Annie.

In March 1941, for unknown reasons, Italian authorities transferred Clara and twenty-seven other German-speaking

Jewish refugees to San Donato Val di Comino in the province of Frosinone, sixty miles east of Rome. Some historians have claimed that the Italians, in defiance of Nazi racial laws, sought to protect Italian Jews and Jewish refugees. While that may have been true in San Donato, recent information indicates that many Jewish foreigners in Italy were interned and shipped to the countryside in a campaign to separate them from the general population.

How the authorities determined where to house the refugees is unknown. My grandmother and two other German-speaking women were especially fortunate. They took up residence in Casa Gaudiello, previously a hotel and probably the grandest house in San Donato. Its owner, Anna Gaudiello, did everything possible to make them feel comfortable and at home.

Clara, Grete Berger, and Grete Bloch each had a bedroom on the top floor. Clara always extolled the fresh air and beautiful rural setting, only expressing discomfort with the lack of central heating.

On April 16, 1941, Clara sent motherly advice related to my father's hair loss.

Hannsel, dearest,

How is it going with your hair? There is a wonderful remedy for hair growth. It contains a vitamin and even helps with hair loss. It is called Ardena or maybe it's orange skin food. It's made by Elizabeth Arden and it has to be rubbed into the scalp at night.

Imagine that in the mountains of Italy, Clara worries about her son's balding and even knows what to recommend!

In June 1941 an opportunity arose that sent her excitement spiraling into the clouds. The Serpapinto, a Portuguese ship proffering transport from Lisbon to America, became the last great possibility for the Spitzers of Ostrava and for Clara. They saw no obstacles to getting tickets. For many Jewish refugees trapped in German-occupied Europe, the ship offered a vision of a maritime Pegasus that could transport them to freedom. The ship carried an almost mythical quality.

From San Donato, Clara reserved a ticket on the August 20 sailing of the Serpapinto. She believed she would reunite aboard the ship with Gretl, Hugo, and Susi. Her letters to my father are dense with details about consulates, affidavits, luggage transport, permits, visas, and documents. Clara had to pack up everything in her room at Casa Gaudiello and ship luggage she had stored in Florence to Lisbon. Money, photos, translations, and medical clearance all had to be arranged.

In a letter to her precious Hans, Clara wrote:

What you are writing about yourself, dearest, is making me very happy. I wish I were already with you. Being alone, it is all so difficult to handle for me. Now it is as you said to me as a little boy. "When I am big and you little again, mother." Now is the time, dearest. I am working hard to gather all my strength. I don't want to be a burden to anyone, only of assistance, this is what I ask of the dear God. Hannerle, I will send a telegram as soon as I have something to report. My sweet, beloved child, I only want to embrace you now with all my heart. I wish you deeply all the happiness and the best. I am looking forward to a happy and healthy reunion with you, with my deepest feelings.

Your Mutti

On June 30, 1941 Clara took the three-hour bus ride to Rome and went immediately to the American Consulate. That very day the consulate had stopped giving out visas. None of the requisite coordination of applications had succeeded. Not the American, the Italian, or the Portuguese. All the money paid with the applications came to nothing. Only the ticket remained, and Clara hoped fervently the money would be refunded to Benjamin Buchsbaum. In her letter to my father, she is philosophic:

Certainly, it was God's will that we will see each other later, and then hopefully we will all be together. May the dear God also keep Gretele and her family healthy and keep them together. I am embracing you and kiss you, my dearest, and thank you for all the love with deepest wishes for your luck and your well-being and your health.

Your Mutti

In her letter of July 16, she reported she had resumed her efforts to emigrate and provided information on Cuba for herself and the Spitzers in Ostrava. She also congratulated 'Johnnie,' my father, on his new suit.

It was very good and reasonable that you complemented your wardrobe. You always have to be impeccable, elegantly dressed, and you should not be beneath anyone. This is how it is; society greatly values it.

She also wrote of suffering with dental problems and consulted with my father about what path to take—replacement crowns or full dentures. Again, lack of money and the necessity to borrow consumed her.

While Europe was two years into World War II, it seems that both Clara in rural Italy and her family in Ostrava were removed from what was happening in other countries. On October 11, 1941 Clara wrote of her deep appreciation for Benjamin and Katherine Buchsbaum and reminded my father to take gifts to both of them and to the younger family members. Her anxiety about asking for money was evident. Her continuing debt to Ben weighed heavily. She was gratified to learn, though, that my father observed his father's *Yahrzeit*.

I hear with deep and inner satisfaction that you spent the anniversary of father's death with piety and that you did not forget to think about him. You well know, dearest, how important this was for father. He who only lived for us and loved us so much, definitely deserved it. Therefore, I thank you for telling me about it. I also lit a candle and Gretl did as well.

On October 20, Clara wrote of a change in the weather:

We had a few cold and stormy days in the mountains that no one dared to go outside. The wind blew through the rooms, and they were freezing cold. I bought some warm underwear for myself since there is no heating provided and only plain windows. Last year it was very harsh. Hopefully it will be milder this year.

She returned to the theme of Norbert's wife Annie, lamenting her impact on the family. She closed with expressions of yearning that grip my heart.

I am already looking forward to your next letter, my dearest Johnerle, your news is my greatest joy. I am thinking so much of you and dream about you, my dearest, which makes me so glad. I only hope and look forward to being together with you again and am waiting for it patiently and steadfastly. Now farewell, my beloved, may all the many and good wishes I have for you come true. Be always happy, joyful and content, and especially healthy. I am kissing you, my dearest, lovingly from the bottom of my heart.

Your Mutti

Hugo and Gretl wrote a cheerful note on October 26, relating that Susi's math team had scored a big win in a competition.

When letters from my father did not come, Clara clearly felt her lifeline slipping away. Perhaps the cold of winter eroded her inner resources. Whatever the reason, her wishes for my father's well-being took on the cadence of desperate prayers.

November 27, 1941

My dearest beloved Hannesle!

I hope that you receive this letter on time for your birthday. I hope that everything I ask God for you, happiness and success, love and beauty, health and joy, and especially everything that makes life joyful and happy, will come true for you without exception. All my thoughts and blessings, my very beloved good child, will be with you on this day, they always find a way to you, they are the goal of my dreams for the future. What do you look like, darling? I sometimes dream about you and the beautiful and happy times when you and Gretele were with me, and then I am sad when I wake up. But it will certainly be better again one day and how happy we will be then together. Then we will be able to value the great joy more than before when we took it for granted. Now you also have to build your own life. May the dear God give you luck, strength and health for it so that you can do it well and may all your activities be blessed. Hannele, my dearest golden child, I embrace you with all my heart, I wish you once again from the good the best and from beauty the most beautiful, now I kiss you with never ending love.

Your Mutti

This was Clara's last letter to my father save one. She did, however, continue to correspond with her brother Norbert who was living in Ostrava.

In 1942 and 1943 she sent four postcards, mostly inquiring about the health and well-being of Gretl and her family and about friends.

She expressed concern about not hearing from Gretl and begged Norbert to provide information no matter what. She also revealed that she had been seriously ill with pneumonia.

> 26./6.43
>
> Liebster Norbert!
>
> Du wirst meinetwegen gewiss beunruhigt sein u. so schreibe ich Dir heute schon selbst, um Dir zu sagen dass es mir schon besser geht. Ich bin schon täglich einige Stunden außer Bett. Die Krankheit nimmt ihren normalen Verlauf aber der Arzt meint, dass es immerhin noch einige Zeit dauern wird, bis es gut wird. Vormittag bin ich schon fieberfrei aber nachmittag habe ich noch Temperatur. Die Dame die Dir schrieb, war und ist mir eine liebevolle Pflegerin die mich wie eine Schwester betreute u. umsorgte u. ihr u. dem unverändert gütigen u. tüchtigen Arzt habe ich es zu verdanken dass ich heute schon so weit bin. Das hohe Fieber durch längere Zeit hat mich ziemlich heruntergebracht u. jetzt wird es schon langsam gehn, bis ich dann wieder zum Hinausgehn kommen. Ich denke an Dich wie Du so vieles besorgen kannst u. bitte Dich, Dir nicht zu viel zuzumuten u. selbst an Dich zu denken. Hoffentlich kommt bald Nachricht von Dir. Ich erwarte sie immer sehnlichst. Meine

47

6/26/43

Dearest Norbert!

You must be very worried about me, and that's why I am writing myself to you today to tell you that I am already doing better. I have already been able to leave my bed daily for a few hours. The illness is taking its regular course, but the doctor said that it will still take some time until I am well again. In the mornings, I am already without fever, but in the afternoon my temperature rises again. The lady who wrote to you was and is a very loving companion who takes care of me and nurses me like a sister would. Thanks to her and to the wonderful competent doctor, I owe them that I am feeling already better today. The high fever, which lasted a while, really drained me, but now it is slowly getting better and soon I can go outside again. I am thinking about you and how you can take care of so many things, and I beg you to not take on too much and to think about yourself. Hopefully, I will soon have news from you again. I am always expecting your letters with much longing. My thoughts are with my children in deep worry because no one is writing, hopefully they are healthy. I am longing for them so indescribably.

Farewell, dear little brother, all my love, I embrace and kiss you, with heartfelt greetings, your sister Clara

The last letter

My grandmother's very last letter, written after April 30, 1943, did not reflect knowledge that her daughter Gretl, son-in-law Hugo, and precious Susi had been exterminated in October 1942 in Treblinka. Did their letters simply stop? Did anyone from Ostrava write to Clara to tell her that they had been rounded up and transported?

These are unanswerable questions. As far as I know, Clara's correspondence with my father in America ended in November 1941, but her correspondence with Gretl and Hugo in Ostrava may have continued.

And yet there was a last letter from Clara, a miracle of a letter, a letter to make me weep, to make my heart stop.

After two and a half years of silence, my parents, who had married on April 30, 1943, received a letter from Clara.

Whether through the International Red Cross or via friends in Switzerland, Clara had received a letter from my father with the news that he had married Eleanor Sanders of Jenkintown, Pennsylvania. He had enclosed a photograph of himself and my mother on their honeymoon in Atlantic City, New Jersey.

In return my parents received a love letter unlike any other. In the letter Clara embraced my mother, who had been motherless since the age of five, and pulled her into the golden harbor of the Buchsbaum family.

Eleanor was welcomed as daughter, sister, and aunt, as well as wife to Clara's precious son, her 'above everything' child.

One of 'The Ritchie Boys'

My father's goal of becoming an officer in the United States Army was finally realized when he was commissioned as a second lieutenant in the Army Air Corps after graduation from Officers' Candidate School in Florida in November 1943. He then served as a legal officer at Camp Springs, Maryland until June 1944.

Subsequently he was sent to the Military Intelligence Training Center at Camp Ritchie in Maryland. The three months of training were to shape his career in the military for the next two decades. In this specialized program, immigrants and refugees, fluent in European languages and experts on the culture of their home countries, became a part of the CIC or Counter Intelligence Corps.

Known as 'The Ritchie Boys,' they employed counterintelligence techniques to gather information as the Allies proceeded across Europe. Twenty-two hundred of them were Jewish. My father's assignment was to find and arrest high-level Nazis.

In August 1944, my father was sent overseas as one of a number of American officers assigned to a British Strategic Intelligence installation in England. One of their tasks was interrogating captured German officers for information about German intelligence activities on the continent. In December 1944, my father was sent to southern Germany as a counterintelligence officer searching for Nazis.

My father never used torture. He said cigarettes and a cup of coffee were the most effective means of gaining information. Uncooperative prisoners were threatened with transfer to the Russian military. This was their greatest fear and led them to reveal everything they knew. The prisoners didn't realize the

Allies would never have put them into Russian hands. This tactic reflected one of the techniques of psychological warfare as practiced by The Ritchie Boys.

I picture my father, by then a captain, being driven by jeep through towns, questioning, interrogating and arresting German soldiers and men in civilian clothes, searching among them for Nazis. The task of discernment, identifying the supremely guilty (SS, Gestapo, and other high-ranking Nazis) from the merely guilty (ordinary soldiers in civilian clothes, Nazi sympathizers, low-level administrators) challenged him.

I wonder if my father ever thought of trying to call my grandmother in San Donato. Was it possible? Did Casa Gaudiello have a telephone? Of course. It had been a hotel.

I imagine a moment when my father gets the idea to call Clara and searches for a phone. His unit always requisitioned the finest accommodations in each town they occupied, liberating wine from cellars along the way. He finds a gold-plated phone on the ornately carved desk in the library of a villa.

"Hallo, hallo. Operator, ja, I want to place a long-distance call to Clara Buchsbaum at Casa Gaudiello, San Donato Val di Comino, Italy. Yes, I can wait." (Sounds of artillery in the background.)

My father drums his fingers on the desk. He is too impatient to sit. Minutes go by. Then, after a long wait, he hears a phone being picked up and words in Italian.

"Per favore," he shouts. "Per favore. Clara Buchsbaum. Prego, senora. Mia madre. Clara Buchsbaum. Mia madre."

"Momento." (Clattering and fluttering in the background. The sound of footsteps running.) And then a voice. Her voice. The voice he has known from birth. A voice not heard for five years.

"Mutti. Mutti."

"Hans? Hans! Hansele. Oh, my son! My son! Oh, my precious boy!"

"Mutti, I am somewhere in Germany. The war will be over soon. We are winning. Hold on, Mutti. Hold on. I will come and find you when the war ends."

"Oh, my Hansel. My darling. My golden child."

The phone goes dead.

My father beats on it, trying to summon the operator.

"Bitte. Bitte. Operator. Operator."

He covers his face with his hands.

It is so little.

It is everything.

In July 1945, a few months after World War II ended in Europe, my father, stationed in Nuremberg, Germany, borrowed a jeep and returned to Ostrava, Czechoslovakia.

He'd gotten permission to leave his post as Chief of the Documentation Section in the American prosecutor's office at the Nuremberg trials to search for his family.

Clara's cherished brother Norbert, along with their sister Sidonia, had survived the war. Miraculously, Norbert had managed to jump off a train bound for Auschwitz. His wife, Annie, then hid him for some time.

Eventually he was rounded up again and spent the rest of the war in Theresienstadt. His sister Sidonia was living in Romania with her daughter.

Norbert and Annie Babad with an unknown child.

Norbert provided the heartbreaking news that Clara had been seen entering a gas chamber in Auschwitz-Birkenau on September 30, 1944. A witness had registered the information at the Ostrava Hall of Records at the end of the war.

How did my father react the instant Norbert told him Clara had died so horrifically? How did a beloved son feel as he pictured his mother's death? The choking on gas. The clawing on one another in the desperation to reach air. The collapse of his mother's soft body, a mother who had loved him absolutely from the moment he was born. The mother he had failed to get to safety. During the ride back to Nuremburg, did he pull over and weep? Did he engage in behavior unbecoming an officer? What was it like living with that grief?

My father wanted to convict Nazis. He was immersed in preparing documents for the Nuremburg trials when my mother insisted that he come home. He returned to the States in July 1946, more than two months before the trials ended that October. Was he reluctant? I think so.

He was always very proud of his time there, where his duties included translating German documents and interviewing captured Nazis.

5 PRIVATE WARS (1952-1996)

Washington, DC - Germany - New York

1953-1960

I still daydream about my Oma Clara, who died on September 30, 1944, three months and seven days before I was born in Washington, D.C. Mostly I wonder what wisdom she would have bestowed on me, her younger granddaughter.

She would be gratified to know how strongly I resemble my blue-eyed father, her precious Hannesl. On my bureau is a photographic portrait of my grandmother in long pearls and a fur wrap that hints at bare shoulders and perhaps even cleavage. Discreet but nevertheless sensual. Her expression is serious, in the style of the early 1900s, before modernity equated a smile with beauty.

Clara Buchsbaum

Gretl and Hans

Another family portrait features my father nestled against the shoulder of Gretl. My father might have been eight. They look pensive and far too serious for the young children they are.

Numerous snapshots of them in a box of Buchsbaum family photos reveal smiles and eyes glinting with love and mischief.

One of my father's greatest gifts to me was his family, embedded in my memory through these black and white photographs and bedtime stories. Years before the word 'Holocaust' entered my vocabulary, I reveled in the imagined embrace of the Buchsbaum family, certain they loved me as much as I loved them. In the way children accept fairy tales as real, I imagined myself as a little girl talking and playing among the relatives in the photographs. It didn't matter that the pictures were taken before I was born. From the beginning, their story was mine.

As an only child who yearned for a sister and a grandmother, I absorbed my father's family through my skin. But I wasn't yet old enough to sort out multigenerational relationships. In my imagination Gretl was my older sister. Gretl's daughter Zuzana, or 'Susi,' became my younger sister. I believed I knew them and talked to them in the German-accented English I was certain they spoke. The fantasy filled my need for a larger family and satisfied my romantic notions of where I fit in the universe.

Sifting through the photos of my father and his sister in their matching sailor outfits—my father Hans, blond and thoughtful, and Gretl, alluring and mysterious with her large dark eyes and tumbling curls, I imagined we played together on the blue oriental rug in Gretl's room. Susi, born in 1931, was part of our trio of little girls playing house with our dolls.

In my fantasy they called me *Liebchen* and tucked me into a canopy bed with royal blue velvet hangings. Cousin Susi and I dressed up in Oma Clara's fancy clothes for our afternoons in elegant European cafes. Sometimes we draped long strands of pearls around our necks and pretended we were going to

Schönbrunn Palace in Vienna to curtsy to the emperor and empress.

Gretl and Hans

I fancied that we lived together, probably in a stone villa, and that Clara was the queen mother, presiding over us and spreading affection and harmony among us all. In style, I think she was a mistress of diplomacy but, at the same time, a fierce partisan when it came to her family.

I wanted to be one of the children dressed in lace and velvet and, later, to waltz in elegant ballrooms with men like my father.

Even today, I indulge a fantasy. I have a very long strand of baroque pearls that I pretend belonged to my grandmother. On rare occasions when I wear them, I imagine myself becoming Clara, entering the opera house in Prague or Vienna, wearing elbow-length gloves and a fur stole.

As I write about my father's family, they become even more vivid, stepping out of the gilded wooden frames that hold their pictures and taking their places on a stage. I picture shifting vignettes and scenes that illuminate the complexity of attitudes and personalities that comprised their relationships.

Zuzana (Susi) Spitzer

Everyone adored and doted on Susi, the only grandchild. Photos show a happy little girl with blonde curls, on skis at an early age, in nursery school, and on Oma Clara's lap. I desperately wanted Susi as my playmate, but I was also envious and competitive. She skied from the age of five and, by ten, was a math whiz. I had a math block, according to my father. Math homework was a nightly horror show with hot tears and foot stamping. I like to think I was literary, excelling in reading, spelling, and writing stories, but my math ineptitude prevented me from attaining a place at the very top of the class.

Comparisons with peers plagued me throughout my childhood so even a photograph could arouse those hateful feelings. But then, in the hot flush of remembering Susi had died in the war, I felt deep shame and remorse.

From childhood I always held out hope that Susi's parents, Hugo and Gretl, had put her on a Kindertransport and that she was alive in England or Scotland, waiting for me to find her. These special trains transported Jewish children from the continent to the British Isles where volunteer families kept them safe. Some children were reunited with their parents after the war. But many parents never returned, leaving their children with only the memory of a hasty farewell as they climbed aboard the trains.

Until 1996 I wondered how my brilliant and all-powerful father could have failed to find Gretl and Susi after the war. Maybe he hadn't tried hard enough. Even after he explained how diligently he had searched, putting up notices with refugee organizations and survivor groups, I still held out hope.

I had long sensed that my father harbored a tinge of contempt for Gretl whom he once dismissively labeled 'café society.' She hadn't gone to university and, in the few years before she married the handsome, successful Hugo Spitzer, she probably met friends for lunch and shopping and perhaps went by train to Prague and Vienna with my grandmother on shopping expeditions. My father saw it as a vain and useless occupation.

Gretl, Hugo, and Susi corresponded with my father after he left Ostrava and arrived in England. A clear bond of affection was sustained in their letters, which centered on the Spitzers' desire to emigrate. Their efforts in this regard were questionable, however.

Gretl and Hugo Spitzer

Seemingly unaware of the necessity to leave as soon as possible, Hugo sought employment comparable to his managerial position at the Vítkovice Iron Works. In his letters to my father and to Benjamin Buchsbaum in Philadelphia, he promoted his qualifications. He sent resumes as far as Canberra, Australia. He seemed to rely on those who already had gotten out. Hugo and Gretl's letters were notable for their lack of urgency and, at one point, Gretl actually wrote, "It's not convenient for Hugo to leave right now."

News came that the Spitzers had moved from Ostrava to the countryside where Gretl had taken up knitting by machine and Hugo worked on a construction crew. Clearly, they were no longer living in their comfortable apartment at 24 Střelnice in a fashionable section of the city. Hugo had lost his job when all Jews had been dismissed from the Vítkovice Iron Works, losing also pensions and other benefits. The family converted to Catholicism, not out of religious conviction but to increase their chances that the Germans would leave them alone. Their conversion precluded the possibility of emigrating to *Palestina*, or Palestine, which some refugees had managed to reach. Had they considered that?

Hugo and Gretl rejoiced when my father arrived in Philadelphia and hoped cousin Ben could bring them over as well. Susi appended one of Gretl's letters with her anticipation of meeting her cousin 'Jane' ("Jean" actually), the daughter of Ben and his wife Katherine.

Dear Uncle Jonny!

I miss you so much. I also would like to see Jane soon. How was her report card? I had a good one. I spent the whole day on the schoolyard where we can play so nicely.

I kiss you many times, Your Susi

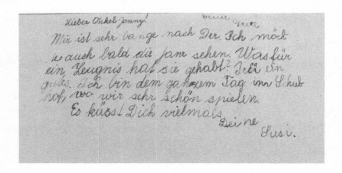

On October 26, 1941 Hugo wrote:

Dearest Johnny!

We were so happy about your letter dated 10/12; we think and talk about you often and hope that all your efforts and work will allow you to enjoy success. We are very grateful to you for working so hard on our behalf; you will certainly also be fruitful here. Based on the entrance permit, nothing stands in the way of our leaving the country.

Hugo did not seem to realize that getting an 'entrance permit' was difficult, if not impossible. Soon after he wrote these lines, U.S. immigration law required a three-year wait.

His own brother, Leo Spitzer, known as Laschi, had reached New York and continued in his role as financial adviser and accountant for the Rothschild family. Yet he refused to sponsor Hugo and his family, which would have been the natural thing, given his secure footing and resources.

Laschi could not fathom that my father was penniless in the United States and dependent on Ben Buchsbaum for room and board as he started a business. "You're a rich man," he told my father. "You sponsor them." The Spitzers, exterminated a year after Hugo wrote about the entrance permit, didn't have three years to wait.

I don't think my father knew their exact end although he mentions in an affidavit written after the war that they predeceased his mother. Perhaps his Uncle Norbert provided that information. Without question, my father and our cousin Ben Buchsbaum in Philadelphia worked very hard to rescue Clara, Hugo, Gretl, and Susi before the Holocaust consumed this beautiful family.

Not until 1960 did my father cut off all association with Laschi and his wife Susi, who lived a luxurious life in a river view apartment on Manhattan's Upper East Side.

I'm sure that long overdue act helped relieve whatever sense of guilt my father felt by sustaining association with Hugo's self-absorbed, uncaring brother. Perhaps no amount of money could have saved Hugo, Gretl, and Susi, but I certainly felt, even as a teenager, a taint in our continued relationship with the Spitzers.

In my wishful imagination today, I picture Susi alive and living in London. I first find her in an outdated TIME magazine. An article mentions her as part of a team grappling with a theory of economics. I could not have imagined the sheep farm in the north of Scotland nor the doctorate from the London School of Economics. My cousin Susi is surprised, stunned actually, when I reach her by phone at her London home. Although she remembers that her Uncle Johnny had gone to America, she never knew of my existence.

"I have been waiting many years for someone to come," she says, with a slight accent I can't identify. "Almost my entire life." Her tone carries a sense of wonder as if she only now realizes seven decades have elapsed.

"I've been searching for you since I was a little girl," I answer. "You were my first hero and I wanted you desperately."

We agree to meet for tea at Brown's, a venerable hotel emblematic of intellectual, literary London. Virginia Woolf could have been a regular. Am I trying to impress my cousin by suggesting Brown's?

We meet the next day. In my handbag I carry the article and some photographs. I am not surprised by my casually elegant cousin. She is tall and slim, dressed in cream-colored cashmere pants and a matching turtleneck sweater. Her silvery blonde hair still boasts the curls of her childhood. My cousin looks fifteen years younger than her eighty-five years.

Susi's story unfolds. Her parents had placed her on the very last Kindertransport from Czechoslovakia, after all, and promised to meet her after the war. When she was eleven, an immensely kind and large family took her in.

"When the war ended, they wanted to adopt me," she says, hesitating, "but I could not give up my identity, my connection to my family.

After a few years, I accepted that they had not survived but I was still of them. They were my everything."

I open my bag and the envelope of pictures spills onto the white tablecloth. She picks up the pre-war photo of herself at eight years old, smiling merrily. Her fingers touch the studio portrait of three generations, taken several years earlier—Oma Clara, her mother Gretl, and Susi on her Oma's lap. Our Oma's lap. Family. Three generations bonded by love. Tears stream from the corners of her eyes. She makes no effort to dry them.

"You see, they did come back, after all. They came back. Just as they promised."

Her trembling hands reach for mine.

"My dearest Barbara, my dear, dear cousin, you are the gift of this day. You are a messenger from my lost life and you have brought back my family. All these photographs. It's a miracle."

I grope in my pocket for a handkerchief and feel a cosmic shift, an upward expansion. I had come to London out of my own childhood need, in search of family for myself, never considering how I would be received or that my presence could be a "gift." We sit in silence. There is so much to share but I sense the essential has already been given and received.

* * *

In 1953, eight years after World War II ended, I moved from Washington, D.C., to Heidelberg, Germany, with my father and my mother. I was eight years old. We went wherever my father's eighteen-year career as an Army officer led us. After three years in Heidelberg, we moved to New York, then Baltimore for a year, and, when I was fifteen, to Berlin, Germany.

In those years, I remember feeling his soft wool jacket against my cheek. The aroma of his Dunhill pipe tobacco and Yardley's aftershave enveloped me in a mantle of security. We loved each other greatly. He could get angry, rarely at the people he loved but frequently at world leaders who made bad decisions that imperiled world peace or American sovereignty. At those times his pipe became a baton, underscoring his diatribes. My father was often adamant. Some considered him arrogant.

I knew from a young age that his great capacity to love me, my mother, and our dogs came from his mother's immense love for him. Such devotion does not develop in a vacuum.

As we neared Heidelberg, I saw bombed out buildings without facades. I can still feel the shock of such devastation just a few miles from where we lived. Fearing for our safety, I found it difficult to fall asleep at night. My parents reassured me that the war was over, but I knew this destruction was bigger and more powerful than any living person.

The years when we lived in Heidelberg, when I was seven to ten years old, became an amalgam of exciting opportunities and emerging fears that lived inside of me.

In Heidelberg, I absorbed knowledge of my father's lost family. Did I learn the words concentration camp? Gas chambers? I don't remember.

I knew the family members in the pictures had died in the war and, eventually, learned they'd been killed by the Nazis. I must have been told that my grandmother died in Auschwitz, but I don't remember when or how. The emphasis was on our family's vibrant lives and my father's assurances they would have loved me.

The author and her parents

He wasn't evasive or silent about family trauma and loss. I feel certain though, that my father was very careful because I was a sensitive, emotional child. He didn't want to traumatize me. But children inhale information and become expert weathermen, taking the emotional temperature of the adults around them. I knew my family was different because we were Jewish and my father spoke with an accent. In our years in Heidelberg I became aware of my Jewish identity. There were no other Jewish children in my grade during our time there.

My classmates asked, "What are you? Protestant or Catholic?" My jaw tensed as I tried to form the 'J' sound. I flushed with shame that I was Jewish and then felt guilty about my feelings. Did being different mean I was inferior? Ten years later I certainly felt that way when I learned Jewish girls couldn't be debutantes or join the Junior League.

Once my neighbor in Heidelberg, Jeannie Jackson, kicked my shins with her oversized saddle shoes and taunted, "Your father should be kicked out of the Army and killed because he's Jewish." Sobbing, I ran home. I thought I really could lose my father, my protector and my stability. Life without him was unthinkable.

That was the first of several antisemitic incidents in my childhood, creating decades of ambivalence about being Jewish.

"Turn the other cheek," my mother advised. "Don't let them know you care." My mother viewed my reactions as somewhat self-dramatizing. She may have been right. While I seethed with righteous anger and then felt superior to my unenlightened classmates, I was only being hurt with words. But hateful language wounds and, unchecked, can lead to harmful actions.

My mother was American and, I think, she felt dislocated and lonely in Heidelberg, so far from her father and two sisters in the United States. Also, the move overseas may have reactivated an episode of depression. I remember her playing Chopin waltzes on the piano on dark winter afternoons, hour after hour, and reading novels while sitting up in bed and smoking one Chesterfield cigarette after another.

As an adult I learned that my mother had experienced a severe trauma when she was five: her mother committed suicide. The event, as well as the loss of her mother, left her with a veil of melancholy. While she was a wonderful mother and companion and could be witty and full of fun, her large gray eyes carried the faraway, forlorn look of an abandoned child.

Despite her fears and anxiety, my mother taught me how to take the streetcar so I could go to ballet class by myself. She took me shopping on the *Hauptstrasse* (Main Street). In a store similar to Woolworths, we shopped for small pots, pans, and dishes for my toy kitchen. Doll-size fruits and vegetables were made out of marzipan, a special almond candy famous in Germany. I never liked the taste.

One of my favorite pastimes was opening the cardboard box that contained the pictures of my father's family. I saw my Aunt Gretl and her changing hairstyles, first long and curly, then short and straight. I looked at Susi with her blonde curls and felt simmering envy. I had straight, coarse hair, good for braids, but my mother tried to turn me into a curly-headed daughter with a hateful permanent. In my heart I knew curly hair was better. My mother and I argued frequently about my hair and clothes. She made me wear white gloves and a hat to Temple.

Every Friday we went to Sabbath services. On Sunday mornings I attended Sunday school while the parents feasted on bagels and played Scrabble or Bridge. We weren't in a synagogue but rather in a building with space reserved for Jewish families in the military. How happy it was having the parents and children all together on Friday evenings and Sundays. I learned Bible stories from the Old Testament. On Purim I dressed up as Queen Esther in a white sheet, like a toga. I wore a golden crown. Being with the other Jewish children felt comfortable.

On weekends my father and I, and our boxer, Becky, sometimes walked through the woods to the *Schloss* (castle), above the city. Before we moved from our Arlington, Virginia, apartment to

Heidelberg, I was afraid of dogs. My father promised we'd get a boxer puppy in Germany. He said I would love her, learn to take care of her, and not be afraid of dogs anymore. Just as he promised, he turned me into a dog lover.

The walks with my father, and our conversations as we climbed the hill to the Schloss, enhanced and solidified our relationship. Five years earlier, when my mother was briefly hospitalized for depression, my father had become, in my eyes, the more stable, protective parent.

During that time, I played with my first friend, Diane, at her family's apartment across the hall from ours. Her grandmother, who introduced us to arts and crafts, took good care of us. Still, my ear listened hard for my father's steps coming up the stairs. I threw myself into his arms every evening and he lifted me up for a big hug.

"How's my little pussycat?" he would ask. I would then press my cheek against his wool uniform jacket and inhale his scent. I was five years old and, with my father, felt a sense of security in the marrow of my bones that lasted until he died in 1988. His absolute love and support, bestowed on him by his mother Clara and passed down to me, is also evident in the patience and tenderness of my son Andrew with his children, Asher and Elia.

The Heidelberg years brought opportunities that grew into enormous gifts that shaped my life. I studied ballet with Madame Tatiana Savitskaya, a Russian refugee from Kiev in the Soviet Union. As the Soviet Army marched west across Eastern Europe in the last months of the war, Madame raced ahead of them, stopping only when she reached the safety of Heidelberg. There the former ballerina opened a studio where German girls, and later the daughters of United States Army officers, met to learn classical ballet fundamentals. While the German mothers may have resented the privileged Americans, everyone got along overall. One German mother generously made my costumes for our performances.

Wanting to transmit his love of horses, my father also arranged for riding lessons at a stable run by an old Prussian cavalryman who wore a monocle. As the first lesson ended, the instructor taught me to do a backward somersault off the horse. We ended every lesson that way. Soon I was cantering without holding the reins—another confidence-building opportunity. I think my father was passing to me his embrace of life and new experiences. Perhaps he also was tempering the possible effects of my mother's anxious depression, which colored her way of being in the world. I didn't know for almost fifty years that my paternal grandfather also had battled depression.

Both my grandmothers and one of my grandfathers died before I was born. When I asked my father why some Jews don't believe in an afterlife, he explained that we continue to live in the memories of those who loved us. "That is our immortality," he said. From a young age I embraced the power of remembering my family.

When I was about ten, my father let me use his black, portable Royal typewriter. He taught me to carefully change the ribbon and clean the keys. My father had earned a Doctor of Jurisprudence degree at Charles University in Prague using that typewriter. The old Royal had quite a history: when it arrived in America, my father had its letters converted to English but left the Czech accent marks over the numbers in the top row. It accompanied him through three years of coursework for his doctorate in history at Georgetown University.

My father taught me to craft prose the way a sculptor molds clay. He passed down the pleasure and challenge of precisely shaping language to convey thoughts. He said there was almost always a better way to say something. I also learned that words and the vehicles we use to record them are agents of transformation.

My parents' determination to give me everything made me a privileged child. The opportunities they provided while we lived in Heidelberg—lessons in ballet, ice skating, piano and horseback riding—were possible because of the post-war German economy.

My parents were abundantly generous in every way, giving me far beyond what my friends' parents provided for their children. Their generosity of time and effort, affection, encouragement and comfort never faltered.

When we left Europe in 1955, I studied at George Balanchine's School of American Ballet in New York City and performed in the Nutcracker at City Center for two years. My parents never complained about getting me home after the late night performances. So much love. "When you're happy, we're happy," my father crooned. "You are the center of our lives."

With all that love, how could I relate my fears to my parents? How could I worry them for even a minute? I had nightmares and a facial tic. I struggled with worries about popularity and never felt pretty or smart enough. I was just so scared, and I couldn't tell them because I didn't want to burden them.

I continued feeling shame about being Jewish, too, and then was ashamed of myself. I was an insecure child who became competitive and a leader of my peers. Nevertheless, I seemed trapped by comparisons with other girls who seemed prettier and smarter.

For me, love came with a mandate to be happy. There is so much pressure to be wonderful when your parents' happiness depends on it. I was trapped by my dependence on my parents; their love was oxygen. But I was also always struggling for freedom. In Heidelberg I madly pedaled my bike, almost always on the sidewalk, and loved the wind on my face. I climbed trees and ignored my mother's pleas to come home. "Barrrrrbie! Barrrbie!" she called. "Time to come home." I ran like the wind until my lungs felt like they'd collapse. That's how I escaped from my fears and the weight of being so loved—the weight of my parents' worrying about me, my health and safety, my schoolwork.

Once I even packed my ballet bag, put Becky on a leash, and ran away from home. We walked down a dirt road that divided the farmers' fields. I had learned in Sunday school that we had to throw away all the bread in our house for Passover—every crumb. My parents said we couldn't because our German maid had a right to eat bread. After I ran away, they capitulated. We threw away the bread and swept up all the breadcrumbs.

I still sensed my mother's ambivalence about being Jewish, though. More than once I overheard her urge my father to change our name to 'Barclay.' He refused. He was proud of being Jewish and insisted he would never deny it. At the same time, they nagged me, "Don't talk with your hands." The message was, "Be Jewish but don't act Jewish." It was very confusing.

My father was embarrassed by, even ashamed of, Hasidic Jews in their tall hats, long black coats, and beards. He had no sense of brotherhood with them, which derived, I think, from a disdain for Jews from Eastern Europe. Czechoslovakia, while contiguous to Poland, had no tradition of Yiddish language and culture. My father and most other German-speaking Jewish refugees felt superior to those who so publicly proclaimed their Jewish identity in dress, language, and Orthodox religious practice. I was embarrassed by father's stance about this.

At home the atmosphere was frequently serious and sometimes heavy. My mother could be witty, playful, and fun, but her expression also could reflect the abandonment she felt in the deepest regions of her being. She seemed to ask: *Do I have a place here? Do I belong?* She compensated by being beautifully and tastefully dressed and applying makeup subtly and effectively. Her hair and nails, which featured red polish and clear half-moons at the cuticles, were done on Fridays. She was elegant. Her two sisters used the word 'smart.' All three dressed in Chanel-style suits and wore choker strands of pearls and pearl or gold button earrings.

I carried my mother's questions of belonging throughout my childhood. They were tied up in knots with my Jewish identity. While my father's voice made me feel loved and secure, my American classmates pointed out his accent wherever we lived. "You're Jewish?" they asked.

I wanted to belong, to be the same but also different. I was a little ballerina show-off, a snob. They were philistines who'd never heard classical music or seen an opera or ballet. My father had two doctorates and spoke at least three languages. We traveled to different countries every school vacation. Yet their questions always hit home, "You're an only child? Oh." "You don't have a grandmother? Everybody has a grandmother." "Is your father a Nazi? He talks just like one." My fingers went around the neck of that girl. Red hot rage consumed me. I banged her head into the playground blacktop. How dare she? That day I felt I had the capacity to kill. My friend Oakley pulled me away. I was eight years old and short and skinny.

The weight of loss on both sides of the family sometimes felt palpable and was connected to the weight of making decisions. Making the right decision could be lifesaving, as it was when my father escaped from Czechoslovakia. Accordingly, his exhortations carried an almost life and death quality. I felt pressure from my father to already know the answer in class, to understand, not to make mistakes. The idea of learning from mistakes did not exist for him or me.

I believe this urgency to make the right decisions harkened back to my father, grandmother, and the Spitzers not taking the train to England during the three-day allowance for immigration without a visa. It recalls Clara not going to South America because she heard the air there was bad for the lungs of the elderly. These had turned out to be fatal decisions.

I never burdened my parents with my upset—my fears, my shame. I knew they couldn't soothe my terror for their well-being. Recurrent nightmares started in Heidelberg. They came when I had a fever deriving from ear infections, measles, and normal childhood illnesses. Occasionally a particular one recurs. I dream I'm in an immense edifice, almost as large as the Colosseum in Rome. It's covered by a roof. Inside are multiple staircases, hidden corridors, and dead ends. I'm running away from danger, lost and desperate to make my way to safety. I don't know which way to head on the staircases. Up? Down? Even describing the nightmare upsets me.

Another fear related to amputations. After the war many men had only one leg. Seeing them terrified me. I feared that could happen to my parents, maybe even to me. The images haunted my thoughts—day and night.

I ran away from my fears by acting fearless—hanging upside down on the monkey bars, climbing trees, pedaling my bike as fast as I could. I was the leader of the neighborhood girls, deciding what we should play and who would be the boss, teacher, or director. We staged plays and performed outdoors, played house (I was always the little girl), jumped rope, and played hopscotch endlessly.

The kids I liked best didn't feel driven to be at the top. They were just nice, relaxed, and happy to let me take the lead. They felt safe. In the cruel capriciousness of girls on the playground, Diane, Pam, and Oakley were loyal. Diane and I have maintained our friendship for seventy years.

Some of the same themes swirled through my life even after we moved back to the States. In 1958, in a new school in suburban Baltimore, the students asked, "What are you joining? MYF or CYO?" Seeing my blank look, they explained: "Methodist Youth Fellowship or the Catholic Youth Organization?"

"Neither," I replied. "I'm Jewish."

Suddenly, twenty ninth-graders walked around me in a circle.

"What are you doing?" I asked.

They said they'd learned in Sunday school how to identify Jews. They were looking for my horns and tail. This took place thirty-five miles from our nation's capital.

I learned my mother's family was one of only two Jewish families in her town. When socializing started around age sixteen, she recalled being invited to a country club dance. Inside the entrance was a big sign: NO JEWS OR DOGS ALLOWED. She asked her date to take her home. He protested. "They don't mean you!" he said. She insisted. Bravo to my mother! Almost a century after the incident, I celebrate her courage and adamancy.

In 1959, my father was transferred back to Germany, this time to Berlin for a year. Soviet troops stationed just a few miles from downtown Berlin, in the Russian sector, were an omnipresent threat that created fast living and a mood of excitement in the city. While Berlin at that time was divided between West Berlin (free and democratic) and East Berlin (Communist), residents of both cities traveled from one sector to the other, commuting to their jobs. Our neighbor and piano teacher Herr Pasch was the pianist for the East Berlin Opera and was one such commuter. While many American teenagers crossed over into East Berlin by S-Bahn, an above ground commuter train, my father forbade me to join them. His work in military intelligence and the fact that he had carried Czech nationality before World War II made him a potential target for a Soviet engendered 'incident.'

In Berlin, my father served on the Allied Staff, a compendium of American, British, and French officers preparing emergency measures in case the Soviets invaded West Berlin. My father, who was not ideologically bound to the old regimes, proudly embraced democracy and the United States. But he still carried a formality that recalled old-world manners, which equipped him to meet and work with diplomats and high-level military officers from other countries. The officers on the Allied Staff went horseback riding on Wednesday afternoons. Weekends brought socializing among the international staff and their wives, and formal events such as the French Officers' Ball.

Sometime during that year, I sneaked out of our house for a date with a German boy. We went to the *Eierschale*, or Eggshell, jazz club. As soon as we got on the trolley car, an almost paralyzing sense of wrongdoing enveloped me. I was betraying my grandmother, my Aunt Gretl, and my cousin Susi. I ended that experiment in international dating as quickly as I could. I had never heard a single pejorative word in my family against German people, yet I knew I'd done something egregious.

One Sunday in Berlin, my parents gave a brunch where I was introduced to a French colonel and his wife, a viscountess. Shaking hands with aristocracy intoxicated me for days. A British major and his wife had a castle in Ireland. They became close friends of my parents for many years. My parents took me, whenever possible, to receptions where I'd socialize with multi-national military and diplomatic members of the West Berlin community.

In May of 1960 the Russians shot down an American U-2 spy plane. The pilot, Francis Gary Powers, was captured and imprisoned in Russia. This precipitated an international incident that was embarrassing for the United States government and potentially destabilizing for American-Russian relations.

The day after the incident was Armed Forces Day. The Americans held a big parade and then hosted a reception in the garden of the Officers' Club. Soviet officers from the Russian sector of Berlin joined the British, French, and Americans and their wives. The tension was palpable. The Russian wives, who probably did not speak English, or were instructed not to socialize, clustered under a tree looking uncomfortable in their flowered dresses. A Russian colonel downed shots of vodka as he lectured my mother and me on how Americans ruin vodka by mixing it with fruit juice. His sardonic smile, triumphant in the face of Soviet victory, held a horrid fascination for me. I felt my mother's arm around my waist, pulling me closer to her. I don't know which of us was more anxious. I was fifteen years old. Next to these events, the ordinary life of an American teenager carried no appeal.

In 1961, back in the States, vestiges of McCarthyism endured in our government, which feared that military inductees might become tools of the Soviet Union and spill all our secrets. In 1962 my father was asked to testify before the United States Armed Services Committee, a Congressional Committee, on a crucial question: should the United States indoctrinate its new military recruits against Communism? He strongly opposed this endeavor. He rejected indoctrination of any sort, believing that educating young people in how to think, analyze, and evaluate would equip them to resist all forms of demagoguery and brainwashing.

He did, however, believe that the Soviet Union represented a threat to national security. He stated in his testimony that Communist cells existed in the United States, many of them in the New York area. Members preyed on disaffected young people who were outside of the mainstream. The quest for inclusion and acceptance by some marginalized youth left them vulnerable to incursions by committed Communists.

My father reiterated to the committee that his expertise did not extend beyond Army recruits and emphasized his view several times that education, not indoctrination, was the best bulwark against efforts by foreign powers to gain a foothold.

Reading his testimony more than sixty years later takes me back to growing up in the Cold War era. We had regular 'duck and cover' bomb drills in school and were besieged by posters proclaiming 'Better Dead Than Red.' My friends and I agreed we'd rather be red. I am struck by my father's flawless responses to questions that danced around the edges of provocation by the committee members. They appeared to have an agenda to institute indoctrination and my father, always respectful, maintained his stance which derived from years of experience as an intelligence officer. His tone was confident and assured.

I am shocked, though, that my politically liberal father shared the committee's concerns about Communist infiltration into American society. I understand that his expertise had been honed over almost twenty years of immersion in Cold War issues, but I also remember his commenting about some colleagues: "They see a Communist hiding under every bed." While my father took seriously Soviet attempts to recruit young army inductees, he never doubted the common sense of most of our youth and the basic health and strength of American democracy.

Reading my father's words in the Congressional transcript gave me his unique voice and this produced feelings of longing for him.

Alone with the past

During *glasnost* in the late 1980s, documents the Soviet Army had confiscated during World War II were released. They'd been taken as its army moved west across Romania, Poland, Hungary, Czechoslovakia—all the countries the Germans had occupied. Meticulous recordkeepers, the Nazis had documented the roundups of Jews and other 'undesirables' and recorded their ultimate destinations.

In 1990 I submitted a search request to the International Red Cross for information about my father's sister, Gretl, and her family. (See Appendix.)

I felt frustrated and regretful that I hadn't discussed my father's family with him in any depth once I had matured. In my twenties and thirties, I raised my children and worked full-time as a teacher. In my forties I worked on a graduate degree and wrote articles about dance and arts programs for the New York Times, New Jersey Weekly section. My father carried those articles in his pocket to show his colleagues in academia and any neighbors he could waylay. My success as a writer gave him such pleasure and pride.

Toward the end of his life, my father expressed the wish that *his* father, Ignatz, could have known what a success he'd been with three major careers—book publisher, American military officer, and Professor of History at Pace University. Yet he never wrote in his family history—or told me—about his father's suicide. Why? Did he feel shame? Was he protecting me?

Of course, my mother's family kept secrets around her mother's suicide, which followed five years of what psychologists then called *melancholia*. Later that term evolved into manic depression and is now known as bipolar disorder.

A family history of depression on both sides comprised a genetic load that may have greatly concerned my father. When we talked in my teenage years, we agreed I was strong like him and his mother. We believed we could meet life's challenges and triumph over disappointments and setbacks, always emerging energized and confident in our ability to fashion a life of meaning and purpose. The unspoken message, of course, was that my mother was more fragile.

However, he also taught me great compassion for my mother. No doubt he saw that her recurring depression sometimes made me impatient with her. Overall, I had a very tender, loving relationship with my mother. Her generosity and support were boundless. Nevertheless, I sometimes behaved like the self-centered adolescent I was.

"Try to understand," my father pleaded whenever I became frustrated with her red-rimmed eyes or irritable mood. "She can't help it." I learned those lessons well, eventually becoming a clinical social worker at forty-eight years old and subsequently working with many clients with bipolar disorder.

My mother's struggles with depression—abetted by heart and pulmonary conditions worsened by cigarette smoking—transformed into full-blown manic episodes requiring three hospitalizations. Her later years were etched by physical and psychological struggle. My father had borne the brunt of her mood swings from 1969, when she first experienced mania, until his death. The initial episode coincided with menopause for my mother and the birth of my second son, Andrew.

In between episodes of deep depression and manic highs, my mother was glorious. After my father died, she continued living in her home and managed every aspect of her life with efficiency and grace. Her neighbors and the town tradespeople adored her because she was extremely generous and very thoughtful.

Ultimately, I achieved great patience with my mother and became the mother of our duo, as she grew more and more emotionally dependent in her later years. We shared many happy times, including occasional summer weekends at the beach, weekly lunch and shopping dates, and outings to Broadway shows.

When I found my mother lying on her bedroom floor one evening and touched her icy shins, I knew depression had won. All my vigilance had failed to protect her from her own self-destructive impulses. Her physical health struggles and relentless battle with her psyche were just too difficult to bear. At last she found the peace she so dearly craved.

After she and other loved ones died in 1995 and 1996, and there was no one left from the older generation, I began mourning not only recent losses but also the loss of my father's family. There was no one left to provide solace.

6 KADDISH

Czech Republic - Poland

2008

In September 1996, six years after I'd filed my paperwork request with the International Red Cross, copies of the deportation documents for Aunt Gretl, Uncle Hugo, and Cousin Susi were placed in my hands. They burned my fingers as I read dates and transport numbers—the Spitzer family's direct line from life to death. The words seared my psyche: Terezin. Treblinka. According to the files of the International Red Cross, "Transport B signified a death transport since less than 10% of the deportees returned after the war." (see appendix).

Theresienstadt (Terezin in Czech) is a small town forty-five miles north of Prague in the Czech countryside. The Nazis converted what had been a military post into a holding camp for Jews destined for extermination. Theresienstadt exemplified the success of the Nazi deception, demonstrating to the International Red Cross that they treated Jews humanely.

Theresienstadt boasted an art studio for children and adults, an orchestra (Auschwitz had one as well), drama productions, and a newspaper. Behind closed doors the reality was an overcrowded, unsanitary concentration camp where disease ran rampant while prisoners waited for transport to Auschwitz, Treblinka and other camps where certain death awaited most.

In 2008, twelve years after I received the deportation documents, I traveled with my sons, Andrew and David, to the Czech Republic. In the old Jewish section of Prague, we found the names of Hugo, Gretl, and Zuzana Spitzer embossed on the walls of remembrance in the Pinchas Synagogue. Their names are listed in the section on Moravia since Ostrava is in the province of Moravia.

In Ostrava we met Michal and Libuše Salomonovič, a couple who continue to occupy a place in my heart for their gifts of self during our time there. Michal, a tall, stately man with a full head of silver hair, had survived labor and concentration camps as a teenager during the war. He and his wife, a genealogist, archivist, and historian, escorted us around the city. Libuše carried in her head and on tiny squares of paper information about my father's family that we could never have unearthed ourselves.

We visited my father's gymnasium or high school, the main city square, and a memorial to Ostrava's Jews who did not survive the war.

Michal and Libuše also took us to the Jewish welfare office, created to help Ostrava's remaining one hundred Jews, most of them elderly. One room had been turned into a remembrance center with a few religious artifacts, an Ark containing a Torah scroll, silver candlesticks, and a Hanukkah menorah. A pastel portrait on one wall looked familiar. I recognized Susi's face immediately from a photo in our family collection. The portrait had been made before the war. After the war former neighbors of the Spitzers had brought the drawing to this office.

Pastel portrait of Susi

I wanted to take it off the wall and clutch it to me. To pack it in my suitcase for my own wall in America. My only comfort is to regard this portrait as representing all the other children tragically cheated of the lives that were their birthright.

The following day we visited Theresienstadt. Inside the entrance of the main building at Theresienstadt, a Children's Wall of Remembrance displays the names of all the children who passed through those doors. We immediately found Susi's name: Zuzana Spitzer. I could not stop crying. Tears blurred my vision as we examined the cases exhibiting the children's drawings.

I looked for Susi's name on the crayon drawings and, later, in the post-war book, *I'll Never See Another Butterfly*. Did she have a chance to make a picture in the time she spent there in October 1942? I longed for some enduring evidence of her time in Theresienstadt, some proof of happy moments. I wanted to hold her hand and reassure her it was only a bad dream, that soon she would be safe in America with Uncle Johnny and her cousin Jean.

Possibly unknown to my father and Norbert, Susi and her parents stayed in Theresienstadt for five days before they were taken to their final destination, Treblinka. Susi was eleven. Old enough to grasp the worst. I hope she had her mother's hand to hold.

My sons and I also retraced the last steps of my grandmother, arriving at Auschwitz in Poland on a hot July day. After we viewed the main Auschwitz concentration camp, we were directed to a second camp, Auschwitz II or Birkenau, a mile and a half beyond. When Oma Clara traveled the final mile of her life over the railroad tracks in Birkenau, she surely carried a sustaining reservoir of love for her daughter Gretl, her granddaughter Susi, and for my father, her 'golden child,' safe in America. Did she know a gas chamber awaited her? That her monumental efforts to avoid capture would evanesce into smoke? Was there another hand for her to hold? These are the questions that lodge permanently in my heart.

We walked under the brick archway into a treeless greensward bisected by railroad tracks that stretched before us. The sense of emptiness and desolation clutched my heart. Gesturing to my sons to keep a distance, I walked on the wooden ties between the iron rails toward a stone and brick structure in the distance, consciously wanting to recreate my grandmother's last minutes, to absorb her aloneness, though there must have been hundreds or thousands there with her.

I kept my eyes mostly on my sandaled feet, picturing her feet next to mine, encased in black, lace-up shoes. Surely my Oma had replaced the elegance of Ostrava with practicality when she fled to Italy. I looked up to gauge the distance and stubbed my bare toe. I embraced the sting. Protectively, I held out my hand to take hers, imagining her beside me and trying, in a very physical way, to fill the emptiness, the sheer absence, of this lovely woman.

Midway along the tracks, the sky darkened, bringing a light mist. By the time we reached the structure, an international memorial with Hebrew prayers and words of remembrance in many languages, my tears and the light rain commingled.

I knew from photographs that the gas chambers were on the left and the crematoria on the right. I walked to the back of the memorial and pressed my forehead against the stone. Sobbing, I thanked my Oma Clara for loving my father with her whole heart and never giving up on him, just the way he loved me. I promised I would remember and love her forever and relate her story to my children and grandchildren. My sons came up behind me, bringing comfort and solace in their gentle embraces.

Today, more than seventy years after her death, I walk with my Oma Clara once again in my imagination, feeling connected to her. I wish she could know that she still matters and will be lovingly remembered.

There was, however, no record of Clara Buchsbaum having been there. I argued with an employee in the newly formed records office. "Where is her name?" I insisted. "She died in Birkenau. A witness saw her entering the gas chamber."

"Please, Madam," he intoned, patiently but indifferently. "We are in the process of compiling an electronic index. It will take time. So many names. It is difficult."

Difficult. He was too young to understand what is difficult. My urgency brought me to the edge of rudeness. The young man explained the elderly were taken directly to the gas chambers, their names not even recorded.

In my psyche this worsened an already nightmarish situation, this attempt by the Nazis to obliterate any record that my grandmother and others had ever existed.

July 2017 Poland

Auschwitz

I felt driven to return to the places where my family had perished. Nine years after my first visit to Auschwitz, I joined a group from my synagogue, Temple Sinai of Summit, New Jersey, on a trip to Poland and Israel.

As before, skies were gray and a sleeting rain fell. It was as if the images captured in newsreels and black-and-white photographs from 1945 had branded the very weather, ensuring sun would never grace this most dark and tragic place.

All of Auschwitz comprises a museum. In one brick building we found an enormous alphabetical list of the Jews killed by the Nazis in many European camps. It extended the length of a room with fat indices on heavy rag paper hung like carpet samples in a rug store.

Insistent, questing fingers plucked at the pages, seeking the names of lost relatives. Groans and exclamations created a cacophony. Did I find my family's names? I cannot remember. My hands shook. Tears clouded my vision.

Rachael Wolensky, a cherished young friend in our group, calmly snapped photos of my family's names. They were there.

Names of Hugo, Zuzana, and Grete Spitzer in the registry at Auschwitz (*Photo by Rachael Wolensky, 2017*)

Our tour bus took us the mile or so to Birkenau. Birkenau. Birch Tree Meadow. An ironic name for these killing fields. And not a tree to soften the barren landscape, though there was some color. Rough green and yellowing grass stretched from the brick entranceway to the gas chambers and crematorium beyond.

As before, I walked along the tracks. Suddenly I was struck by the reality before me. The train tracks extended to the gas chambers. Of course. My grandmother's last walk wasn't a walk at all. She was transported by boxcar right up to the gas chambers. There'd been no time to breathe. To feel the late summer air caress her cheeks. To snatch a glimpse of sky.

Photo taken inside Auschwitz-Birkenau *(Photo by Rachael Wolensky, 2017)*

No time to be afraid? To say a prayer? Did my Oma Clara know her destiny? I hope not. Please. Let her not have known. Not even for a second.

Now, more than seventy years after her death, the brick gas chambers and crematoria have collapsed inward. Time is the ultimate victor here.

We gathered around Rabbi Gershon to read responsively and recite prayers. My voice choking, I told my companions about my grandmother, Clara Buchsbaum, and read her last letter. Her embrace of my mother with loving words reflected the abundant love that resided within her.

Just speaking Clara's name affirmed that she lives on. Her legacy has been passed on to my sons, David and Andrew, and to my grandchildren, Asher and Elia.

We recited the words of Hannah Senesh, a Hungarian poet and partisan who lost her life in the Shoah.

There are stars up above
So far away we only see their light
Long, long after the star itself is gone.
And so it is with people that we loved
Their memories keep shining ever brightly
Though their time with us is done.
But the stars that light up the darkest night,
these are the lights that guide us.
As we live our days,
these are the ways we remember.[1]

Treblinka

The following day we visited Treblinka, where the Spitzers perished. At Treblinka, the earth groaned. At first it seemed like such an innocent-looking meadow until I saw the seventeen thousand jagged stones, a symbolic memorial cemetery.

Here, the eight-hundred thousand exterminated, some of whose ashes were buried in a pit in the center, find their individual and collective voices. I heard their voices and will remember.

Treblinka Memorial Stones *(Photo by Rachael Wolensky, 2017)*

The approach to Treblinka seems as benign as it must have in 1942 and 1943. A path through a lightly forested section opens into a green space where railroad tracks once transported riders ignorant of the camp's true nature.

Some had even purchased tickets in their home city, riding in coach, believing that a labor camp, or place of resettlement, awaited them. Those travelers changed at a nearby junction for the special train to Treblinka. Where railroad tracks once ran, concrete rectangular slabs now form part of the memorial.

A replica of the original station, part of the sadistic deception of Treblinka, fooled those transported until the last minutes of their lives.

Women and children were shuttled to the left, men to the right. A brief time was allotted for the shearing of heads and stripping of clothing. Pieces of string were distributed to tie pairs of shoes together so they could be reclaimed after showering.

First the men, then women and children, were forced to run down a wire-enclosed passage to the unseen gas chambers beyond. Those unable to keep up were escorted behind a building and shot.

By the time the men's bodies were hauled into burial pits, the women and children were entering the death chambers. The entire operation proceeded with incredible efficiency. When the gassing machinery ran well, twelve to fifteen thousand people could be exterminated in one day.

This is where Hugo, Gretl, and eleven-year-old Susi disappeared into ash after being wrenched from their lives and shoved into a boxcar. Their only crime: they were Jewish. Treblinka was the end of hope, the end of life. How could it be? How can it be? From life to this nothing? Only ashes and stones.

When the Polish tour guide explained that sometimes the gassing process faltered and the timetable was disrupted, causing a backup, I stopped listening. I drifted over to some stone memorials with inscriptions in English and Hebrew.

My hand reached out for Susi to hold her back, to comfort her. How could I remove myself if I wanted to bear witness? But how could I endure another minute of gratuitous details? My ears pounded. This felt like the most wretched moment of my life.

Thoughts that still haunt me center on whether Gretl and Susi knew that death awaited. I'm sure Gretl held and comforted Susi until the last breath, but it's the idea of knowing, of anticipating, and feeling powerless, helpless in the face of that knowledge.

And I must live with that specter because there is no certainty, no solace.

As we walked among the memorial stones, Ron, our Israeli tour guide, took my hand. We found the stone with Czechoslovakia etched into it. I could not stop trembling. We lit *Yahrzeit* candles. Between sobs I spoke briefly about knowing my family only through letters and pictures.

Treblinka *(Photo by Rachael Wolensky, 2017)*

Rabbi Gershon led us in prayers beside the enormous stone memorial.

Fully Compassionate God on High
To our six million brothers and sisters
Murdered because they were Jews
Grant clear and certain rest with You
In the lofty heights of the sacred and pure
Whose brightness shines like the very glow of heaven
Source of mercy:
Forever enfold them in the embrace of Your wings;
Secure their souls in eternity.
Adonai: they are Yours.
They will rest in peace. Amen.

Treblinka seared me visually and emotionally, perhaps because I had no preparation for it. I had known Auschwitz from black-and-white photographs, films, and our 2008 visit.

Treblinka blindsided me. The more I learned from our on-site Polish tour guide and my research afterwards, the more horrific the place became.

Treblinka embodied the purest evil embedded in the soul of some human beings. Perhaps all human beings.

Memorial at Treblinka *(Photo by Rachael Wolensky, 2017)*

---

1. Permission granted by the Association of Reform Rabbis for use of the above prayer, September 2019.

7 SAN DONATO VAL DI COMINO

San Donato *(Photo by Andrew Gilford, 2018)*

San Donato Val di Comino

August 2018

A year later I found my Oma Clara at the kitchen table on the second floor of Casa Gaudiello in San Donato Val di Comino, Italy. My visit to the house where she lived from 1941 through 1944 was the culmination of several years of research.

Here she wrote reams of loving letters to my father, detailing her efforts to find a country, somewhere in the wide world, that would open its doors to one stalwart refugee. Here, in 1944, five years of hope and valiant effort ended when she was taken captive and began the brief, final journey to her tragic end.

San Donato *(Photo by Andrew Gilford, 2018)*

On a sunny morning in August 2018 my sons David and Andrew, David's wife Shari, and I walked across the cobblestones of San Donato's main plaza. Three months earlier, I'd written to the town's mayor, Enrico Pittiglio, telling him of my desire to visit San Donato. That day the mayor warmly shook our hands, introducing us to town historian Luca Leone and other local leaders. Over a specially prepared lavish breakfast in the mayor's office, we received general information about the war years and the interned refugees. Everyone seemed to be talking at once, taking our hands, beaming, embracing us. A photographer snapped photos nonstop.

Center stage stood Alfonsa Gaudiello, a well-dressed woman in her eighties, seemingly the town's *grande dame*. She held onto my hand and talked while our translator, Delia Roffo, rendered her words into English.

Mayor Pittiglio had specifically requested Delia, an Italian-American woman from Massachusetts, who grew up in San Donato. I think Delia's heart is embedded in the ancient stones of her hometown though she navigates her Italian and American identities with great spirit. She divides her year between homes in Boston and San Donato.

Today's residents of San Donato, rightfully proud of their history of receiving and protecting refugees, are taking steps to memorialize that history by placing blue markers on houses where refugees found sanctuary.

Blue Marker

Eventually those devices will provide audio information about the San Donato host families and the refugees who found safety with them. An engraved memorial stands in front of the town hall. The local schools now include the Holocaust as a part of their curriculum.

Memorial in San Donato

While the Italian government determined that refugees were to be interned in areas away from cities, many of the people of San Donato extended that edict and offered sanctuary and protection. One risked her own life to forge identity documents for some of the residents. Another woman hid the mother of a newborn in a basket of straw which she placed on her head as she walked out of the village. Her infant, safely hidden in the village, grew up to be Katya Tannenbaum, a professor at the University of Rome.

The author (left) and Alfonsa Gaudiello

After breakfast, with a sense of urgency and tears, Alfonsa led a small group of us up the street to her family home at 5 Via Orologio. There she provided the information I craved, the details of my grandmother's stay.

The original Casa Gaudiello edifice is actually two-facing buildings, three stories each, connected by a wood and glass passageway on the second floor. At ground level the cobblestone lane runs in front of the buildings and beneath the connecting corridor.

Alfonsa Gaudiello was a child in the household during my grandmother Clara's time there. Her mother, Anna Gaudiello, the owner of what had been a large hotel, protected and cared for her three Jewish guests. Alfonsa carried within her memories and stories from the war years. She may have seen and heard things that could have terrified a child. I got the sense this particular story lived close to her heart.

Alfonsa and Anna Gaudiello

When Clara arrived from Florence on or around June 7, 1940, she embraced the fresh air and rural environment of San Donato. She wrote to my father that she had left Florence because the Pensione Balestri was scheduled for renovation. In addition, her residence permit in Florence was not being renewed.

She did not explain that she and other foreigners were rounded up and designated 'interned,' which involved restrictions on their freedom of travel within Italy.

Casa Gaudiello interior *(Photo by David Gilford, 2018)*

We learned that Clara and two other German-speaking women, Grete Berger and Grete Bloch, found refuge at Casa Gaudiello. Grete Berger, who was born in the Czech province of Moravia, had been a silent film star.

Grete Bloch, born in Berlin, had been the fiancée of Franz Kafka and had given birth to his son out of wedlock. The child died in 1921 at seven years old. Some sources say Grete Bloch was Kafka's wife. Clara may have traveled to San Donato with these women, or perhaps she met them at Casa Gaudiello.

We walked through the gracious, three-story home that, in its hotel years, included a similar building across the lane. The furnishings were comfortable and well-chosen, reflecting prosperity and an eye for décor.

Alfonsa explained that the brocade draperies and upholstery on the chairs and couches had been changed since the war, but the furniture, mostly antique, was original to the house. The overall feeling was one of warmth and comfort, with paintings and prized possessions in abundance.

When we got to the kitchen Alfonsa pushed me down into a chair at the long table. "Here, here was where your grandmother sat. Such a lady. You could tell she was a woman of culture." She took her place at the head of the table. "My mother sat here." She recalled brushing my grandmother's hair and helping her put on her stockings. The relationship between them seemed one of mutual fondness.

With a tone of apology, she explained that food limitations allowed for only one meal a day—a vegetable stew mixed with bread. I felt certain her mother would have created something delicious and filling.

Casa Gaudiello kitchen *(Photo by David Gilford, 2018)*

Our tears mingled as we awkwardly embraced across the corner of the table. I pushed aside two layers of colorful woven table coverings and ran my hand over the scarred and gouged country table. I imagined my grandmother doing that as well, stroking the wood with her fingertips—that very same piece of wood in that very spot—to push away worries about her children.

Everything Clara had known in her life in Czechoslovakia was left behind. Her future was uncertain. The good fortune of finding refuge in this medieval town built into the side of a mountain gave Clara comfort, which she expressed in her letters to my father.

There are many stories in and around my grandmother's story. Information hides in corners and cupboards. A secret back stairway and attic provided all too temporary safety. The dark stone basement and upper floors of Casa Gaudiello form archaeological layers. Even the appellations *Casa*, *Albergo*, and 'hotel' attest to the various functions of the structure over decades and perhaps centuries.

Clara bought long woolen underwear to endure the cold winters and somehow received her Persian lamb coat from Ostrava. Ten years after the war, my mother wore a Persian lamb hip-length swing jacket with gold buttons. I always thought it had been my grandmother's but that was a child's wishful thinking, an expression of yearning for something tangible to connect me to Oma Clara. In one letter my grandmother wrote that one of the other women had bought a clay oven to heat her room and that she hoped she'd be invited to play cards in a warm room, as she had the previous year. Of course, she would offer to bring some wood to heat the oven. But the owner of the clay oven had become reclusive and my grandmother wasn't sure she'd be welcomed.

The letters reveal nothing about Clara's relationship with Grete Bloch and Grete Berger. Her focus on social class (and perhaps theirs as well) adds up to an imagined picture of three once prosperous and elegant women, polite but not intimate with one another. Was there competition for the affection of Anna? They were paying five hundred lire a month each for room and board, equivalent to five American dollars at the time. During the war a loaf of unsliced white bread in the United States cost eleven cents.

The town provided a monthly stipend to its interned refugees. My grandmother had to get official permission to leave town before she traveled to Rome to besiege consulates and embassies. She also sought dental care there. At one time she stayed in Rome for several weeks.

Most of the San Donato men had left the town. It's difficult to determine whether they were evading conscription into the Italian army or hiding from the Italian Fascist government. Before the war a number had emigrated to Newton, Massachusetts, leaving the women of San Donato to run things.

On January 11, 1944, the Allied forces launched their first assault on the German stronghold in the nearby town of Montecassino. The fighting was fierce and lasted several months. The refugees were safe until German soldiers at Montecassino came down to San Donato in February and March of 1944 for respite from the fighting. At Casa Gaudiello they danced to music from the record player while Clara and the other women remained in their rooms.

On April 6, 1944, German soldiers appeared suddenly, looking for Jews. Fascists in San Donato had betrayed the refugees and those harboring them. Hiding the refugees became imperative. Clara, Grete Bloch, and Grete Berger were quickly escorted across the passageway to the building on the other side of the street where a hidden stairway led to the attic.

Clara's safety and comfort ended that day, April 6, 1944, when she and sixteen other hidden Jews were rounded up and taken to prison in Rome. The following day they were transported to the Fossoli concentration camp near Bologna, where they remained almost six weeks.

Fossoli Concentration Camp, photo by RanZag,
Creative Commons Attribution-Share Alike 3.0
Unported license.

Photographs of the Fossoli camp are grim. The buildings, probably much deteriorated today, are hardly more than shacks. What was Clara feeling? I imagine her composure and fundamental confidence, which had sustained her since the Nazi invasion of Czechoslovakia in 1939, held her together. Even as she faced the terror of the unknown, she would have kept her thoughts on my father, safe in America with his lovely wife, Eleanor. His well-being meant everything to her.

On May 16, 1944, the three women and several other refugees from San Donato boarded a train to Auschwitz. Clara was in boxcar 10, as were Grete Bloch and Grete Berger. The town historian places Primo Levi, the Italian poet and writer, on the same transport. Written sources, however, offer conflicting information, claiming he was rounded up and transported to Auschwitz in February 1944. Levi, who survived his time in Auschwitz, later wrote of the numbing cold and unbearable thirst on the six-day train ride.

The date of death for Grete Bloch and Grete Berger is recorded as May 23, 1944. There is no date of death for Clara Buchsbaum in the Auschwitz records. There is only that eyewitness who saw her entering a gas chamber on September 30, 1944—the date recorded in Ostrava's municipal records.

My grandmother came so close to surviving. If she died on September 30, 1944, my mother was already pregnant with me. I was born January 6, 1945. Auschwitz was liberated by the Soviet Army on January 27, 1945. I can almost reach out and touch her. So close.

I hope thoughts and memories of family life sustained my Oma Clara in boxcar 10 as it stood immobilized on the tracks in Auschwitz. Did she know Gretl and her family had been exterminated in Treblinka in October 1942? Did mail stop between my father and his mother with America's entry into the war? Or are there simply letters missing from my collection? After all, Clara wrote in the spring or summer of 1943 after receiving news of my father's marriage. These questions have no answer.

Greedily I scan an affidavit provided by my father as part of an application for reparations from the German government. Submitted in September 1957, one section jumps out at me. (See Appendix.) My father wrote:

My attempt to bring my mother to England was destroyed with the outbreak of the war. After Italy entered the war, I found out through Switzerland that my mother had been interned in San Donato, Frosinone, Val di Comino. She had no financial means and lived on the small amounts that friends from Switzerland and Italy transferred to her. After my emigration to the United States in February 1941, I sent my mother whatever I could spare from my meager income. My efforts to bring her to the United States failed again when America entered the war (Dec. 1941). From that time on, I only received two letters through the Red Cross and from a friend in Switzerland. From that time on, I no longer received any news about her until I found out after the war that my mother had been deported by the German authorities to Auschwitz where she lost her precious life in the gas chamber.

My father concluded in the affidavit that "my sister Gretl Spitzer and her daughter Susi Spitzer passed away before my mother's death."

Hearing my father's voice in his documents overwhelms me with longing for him and his family. The starkness of his words amplifies the tragedy. Condensing the larger family story into a skeletal recitation of facts somehow increases the magnitude of loss. The absence of detail is deafening, as if words concerning the tragic deaths of mother, sister, and niece—in fact, their horrific murders—could ever capture all that had been forever lost.

Can I love and cherish my grandmother, my Aunt Gretl, Uncle Hugo and Cousin Susi, known but never met, and then grieve their loss? Every day the sadness rises up. Tears fall. I press my hands, one on top of the other, over my mouth to hold in my sorrow. Perhaps the solitude of aging is part of my grief. The landscape of my life lacks an older generation. I am the matriarch now. But deep inside there is still the little girl who yearned for a grandmother with an ample lap for comfort. My sense of loss is for me but equally for them. With indifference to suffering and justice, with a craven absence of humanity, Hitler and his henchmen sent them to their deaths, leaving the second generation of survivors to mourn their losses and live in their imaginings of horrific endings.

At the same time, though, my tears of sadness are transforming into fulfillment. I know my family to the fullest extent possible. I have embraced their rich legacy and have given that legacy to my children and grandchildren. I can feel happiness beginning to dance around the edges of my being.

I once asked my father if he hated the Germans for killing his family. He hesitated for a beat or two and then, with great seriousness, replied, "Hate destroys the hater." While he didn't answer my question directly, his reply reflected a considered choice not to let the corrosiveness of hatred blight his life.

While many others of the second generation have experienced secrets and silence about their lost relatives, and were left with unanswered questions, I received a full complement of stories and pictures that comforted me and bolstered my sense of identity.

They were there too—Clara and Ignatz, Gretl, Hugo and Susi, and, always, my father. The fullness of their lives and the love I found in their letters live in my heart. Even today, more than seventy years later, they inspire me. Ours is a story of loss but also of enduring love.

I wish my grandmother could know the comfort of my embrace and my deeply felt love. I am now more than ten years older than she was when she died at sixty-two.

She would have enfolded me in her arms, pressed me to her, and marveled at my resemblance to my father. Now it is I, in my imagination, who holds her in her final days.

She continues to live as a guiding star for me—an example of courage, resilience, and grace and an exemplar of the deepest, undying love.

I also hope my father would find solace in my efforts to keep the memory of his family alive. My endeavor has required tenacity and sustained effort, qualities I learned from his example. All I can do now is write him a letter.

Dearest Daddy,

In four days, I will mark your Yahrzeit at Temple Sinai by saying your name and reciting the Mourner's Kaddish. Yes, I do that every year—something you never envisioned. In one of our last conversations, standing in the kitchen on Northumberland Road, there were tears in your eyes when you implicitly blamed me for not giving David and Andrew a Jewish education.

John Buchsbaum

"Who will say *Kaddish* for me?" you asked. I heard the emotion in your voice. Neither of us even considered that I could.

Not only do I say *Kaddish* for you every year, but I say it for your mother, for Gretl and Susi and, with some reluctance, for Hugo, whom I try not to blame for Gretl and Susi's deaths. I say it for Mommy whose life ended so tragically.

I wish you could know that I have told the Buchsbaum family story in high schools and at Temple Sinai. Clara Buchsbaum, your mother, my grandmother, stands as a paragon of love, courage, resourcefulness, and, ultimately, of resilience.

I wish we could talk about the loss of your family and how so much tragedy impacted you. You were always so steady, so strong for us, so affectionate and constant in your loving support. But I wonder how you sustained yourself in the midst of such tragedy. I am writing this letter to you because I want to know where, for the next forty-four years, you stowed your grief over Clara's loss.

I moved a stack of books from your living room to my study more than twenty years ago, never knowing you had stored Clara's letters in a folder among them. The cardboard file folder was securely anchored between the book on Israel and a giant atlas. How ironic, considering her relentless search for sanctuary. I discovered Clara's last letter in your safe deposit box.

I think you packed away the pain of losing her with the letters— not exactly forgotten, perhaps, but safe and waiting there until you were able to read them and finally let yourself grieve. I wonder if your massive and fatal stroke was the culmination of decades of not grieving.

You gave me your family's life in Ostrava, but you didn't give me their deaths. You gave me philosophy, "Hate destroys the hater," but nothing about your grief. You gave me a date, September 30, 1944, the day Clara died in Auschwitz, but not how you felt when Uncle Norbert told you in 1945 when you visited him in Ostra-

I don't say these things with accusation but, rather, with the greatest compassion I can summon.

I imagine you saying, "I had to be strong for you and Mommy. There was never a right time. Your mother was fragile. You were my little pussycat and I had to protect you from heartbreak." That was true, but I grew up. And I never even asked you. Perhaps I was too consumed with my own life, with raising children, teaching, and writing. But now, when I want to ask, to know, you aren't here.

Perhaps you suffered survivor's guilt and blamed yourself for getting out when you could. Mommy thought this might be so, but I'm not sure she was right. From the letters, I can tell how much you gave your mother—your steadfast love and encouragement, your many attempts to provide documents. And you begged and borrowed money for her visa applications and her sustenance. It must have been so humiliating for you to have to ask others for money, principally our cousin in Philadelphia. Your letters to him, asking on behalf of your mother and then promising to repay him, survive in his family archive. I never knew if you repaid the loans, so I made a significant contribution to the United States Holocaust Memorial Museum in Washington, D.C., in his memory. I felt it incumbent on me to clear your name of any indebtedness. I was happy to make the contribution in lieu of the debt even though the donation was significantly less than what was owed.

I think you channeled your grief over your loss into yet more accomplishment. You worked all day at the Historical Division of the Army and then went to Georgetown University at night for an American doctorate. You were a husband and father and yet you finished the coursework in a few short years. I found your excellent grades. I have many of the major papers you wrote for those classes, every one of them earning an A or A+. The professors must have loved having you in their classes.

Occasionally I get a phone call from a former student of yours. One of your favorites wanted the photographic portrait of you, the one an artist turned into an oil portrait for Pace University. I now regret that I gave it to him. It disturbed me to see the beginnings of illness and old age in you. You were a great romantic figure to me. Your accent, your *savoir faire*, your vast knowledge of European history that held your students spellbound—all were part of the father I loved and adored.

I found it painful to watch when you felt yourself losing your power to compel interest, to hold your place top and center in the pantheon of esteemed professors. You became querulous. You just couldn't handle the loss of who you had been.

Buchsbaum House at Pace University *Photo by Anne Bishop, 2019*

Buchsbaum House remains on the Pleasantville, New York campus, now housing the Education Department. The History Department occupies a different building. Several professors at Pace remember your name, even after thirty years. You made your mark wherever you went. Be assured of that.

There is just one more thing I want to tell you. When I went to San Donato with Andrew, David, and David's wife, Shari, in August 2018, I remembered our trip to Italy in 1954. You walked up a little hill and looked over the landscape to what I now know was San Donato Val di Comino where your mother found sanctuary. I couldn't tell from your erect stance the immense weight of your sadness, but I felt it in the silence. You stood, gazing over the fields toward the town, like a general on the top of the hill. I think we were all paralyzed by the grief we felt was inside of you. We stood in silence, too, next to the car. I wanted to run up the hill to hug you.

Your feelings must have threatened all your self-control, the very foundation of your being, and this breaks my heart for you. You could have driven into town and kissed the stones at 5 Via Orologio and wept, as I did. You could have met Anna Gaudiello and her daughter Alfonsa and heard them praise your mother. But it was too much for you. I understand. It's all right. I'm doing the grieving for you now, every time I sit down to write or whenever I talk about the Buchsbaums of Ostrava.

My generation mourns what your generation couldn't allow themselves to do. We grieve as we write and make films and art. We remember and we speak so that our lost loved ones, those we never met but believe we know, will be remembered.

We tell the stories to our children and they to their children. We keep loving the way Clara loved you, in the very marrow of her bones, and the way you loved me. And that is the finest legacy of all.

The last letter of Oma Clara

My very beloved children!

I am still completely under the spell of the joyful news that you, my beloved Hannesl, have gotten married. This message moved me so deeply that I, at first, couldn't contain myself. You must know how deeply I am taking part in your good fortune, my dear child, and how fervent my prayer is that the dear God may always and always preserve it for you. All the dear and beautiful words you write about Eleanor make me so happy and confident, a safe guarantee that you made the right choice.

Where people are brought together with love for each other, complete understanding and deep inner values, they have the foundation for a happy marriage.

You dearest Eleanor, I embrace most warmly, holding you close to my heart, and welcoming you as my dear daughter. I will always love you and be the mother to you that you unfortunately lost so early and had to miss. We will certainly get along well, dearest. We are only a small circle, we love each other deeply and are very attached to each other. Now you, my dear child, will completely belong to us.

Your brother and sister (Hugo and Gretl) will also love you very much and be happy that they have gained a dear sister. Their lives are at the moment very difficult, but they are attached to each other with great love and that helps them to bear the heavy burden more easily.

That you are industrious is meeting with my great recognition and respect. I am convinced that you, dearest Eleanor, will be the good, faithful and loving companion that he deserves. He is an outstanding person with noble character, full of goodness and warmth, and he has always given us much joy. I am already longingly awaiting the photos that you promised. I can hardly wait to get to know you, dearest Eleanor, if only for the moment from the pictures and to see you again, my Hannesle, until there will be a real reunion in not too distant a future.

I am thanking our dear Bens deeply for the great love that they have shown you, my beloved Hansl. I am deeply grateful for the paternal affection of dear Ben. May the dear God reward him many times over because they deserve it. I send them heartful greetings. It is very painful that our beloved Vaterle [father] was not able to share this joy with us. Now it has already been 5 years since we lost him.

Now my very beloved children, again my deepest wishes for a happy, healthy, successful and joyous future and God's abundant blessings. I am also sending greetings to Eleanor's dear father and am happy that he has also become very fond of you, my Hannesle. I am embracing you and kiss you in deepest love. Write soon to your always loving mother.

Mutti

(written after April 30, 1943, my parents' wedding date).

John and Eleanor Buchsbaum on their honeymoon

AFTERWORD

Coming to terms with tragedy is an ongoing process. We don't "get over" our losses but we learn to live with them. When we face and embrace what happened, own and accept the devastation and its impact on us and our individual families, we enlarge and strengthen our own capacities for living. We can create meaning and this helps to heal.

The path to making meaning is personal. Those who have written about their families, made works of art, created memorial scholarships or other bequests, worked to educate others about the Holocaust and participated in a multitude of endeavors, may find emotional fulfillment and a sense of peace. An additional outcome is a deepening maturity of our very selves or, as some would say, our souls.

Writing about losing the Buchsbaum family has been profound. My grief, perhaps inherited, may have been born at the gates of Auschwitz-Birkenau in 1944, three months and seven days before my birth. Does loss get stored like precious letters kept safe between books? Mental pictures of Clara, Gretl, Hugo and eleven-year-old Susi walking into the gas chambers coexist with images of beauty found in nature, in great works of art, and in the faces of babies at the beginning of discovery.

Through writing I preserve my individual family and their place among the six million lost. By naming those who died and protecting and cherishing the photographs, letters, and remembrances of the Holocaust generation, I have made a statement: They lived, they mattered, and, through writing, I memorialize them.

As we make our way, we cannot ignore studies on how trauma impacts the psyches and physical health of immediate victims and successive generations. The inheritance of some second- and third-generation Holocaust survivors includes parents and grandparents who didn't process their trauma or mourn their losses. The legacies passed down by the parent generation may include or engender anxiety, depression, feelings of not belonging or fitting in, even the belief that we do not deserve to be happy.

I believe many children of survivors feel an obligation to be wonderful, to succeed, to compensate for those who were lost. Some believe they were never enough and never stopped dancing as fast as possible. But how wonderful must we be?

Our legacy of the genocide of six million innocent Jewish people includes the challenge of mourning the losses on behalf of our parents who just couldn't allow themselves to grieve. For some, their psyches, perhaps their souls, endured in a state of emotional landlock with no available egress, no gentle easing of barriers into their own deepest feelings. While my parents seemed to be emotionally expressive, I did not ever see or hear them express the deep sadness they must have felt at the loss of their mothers. Both of them could, on occasion, get angry and perhaps that was their defense against grief. My father railed at what he considered naïve foreign policy by government officials but only once at my mother. My mother targeted her two older sisters. Unlike my parents, I was a crybaby and now I wonder if all my tears, deriving in part from my fears, were an unconscious assuming of my parents' unexpressed grief.

Our history comes with a mandate to remember and tell our family stories even when our parents could not. The silence in many first-generation Holocaust survivors—those who survived the camps, those who endured the terror of hiding, and those who escaped and left family behind—surely reflected a determination to protect their precious young children. But the silence also protected the survivors themselves and it came at a price that is also passed down.

Equally important to acknowledge is that first- and second-generation Holocaust survivors have demonstrated remarkable resilience. Many, if not most, have thrived. Post-graduate degrees, stellar professional achievement, and the capacity to raise stable children who also make contributions in science, medicine, education, government, the arts and many other arenas, all reflect the power of hope, expectation and the force of life. In the postwar generation, survivors and their descendants have become social workers, psychologists, and psychiatrists in large numbers.

Holocaust survivors and their descendants have spearheaded and joined movements on behalf of human rights and against tyranny, repression and genocide. Their moral outrage, their capacity for empathy, and their determination to fight injustice wherever they witness it are all part of the legacy of the Holocaust.

Tears come very easily to me and I regard that as a gift. I weep for Clara and Gretl, for Hugo and Susi. I weep for my father, who lost them all. I weep for never knowing a grandmother's love and comfort. But I also allow the discovery of letters, especially my Oma's last letter, to transform tears of sadness into joy. How comforting it is that as I hover somewhere between the autumn and winter of my life, I carry the Buchsbaums from Ostrava with me.

I carry my father's gifts in my genes. Like his mother, he loved with abundance and lived with every kind of generosity. He taught me, in words and by example, the fulfillment of sustained, hard work. When I asserted that I only wanted to be happy, he proclaimed: "Happiness is not a thing you can get. It is the by-product of doing your very best and feeling pride and satisfaction."

The inexorable link between memory and love ensures that we of the second generation will always remember. For me, the mandate of obligation has become a loving choice informed by getting to know my family, reciting their names, and telling their vibrant, courageous stories.

In the end, their lives and their individual, unique selves cannot be eclipsed by the tragedy and circumstances of their deaths. They exist together in life and in death and their memory lives on in our very cells and in our souls.

APPENDIX

1938: Business card of Hanns Buchsbaum, I.
Buchsbaum publishing company

1939: "Ministry of the Interior: demography and race"

I, Clara Babad-Buchsbaum, of Sigmund, widow of Ignaz Buchsbaum, born in Bielsko on 1/7/1882, a Jewish-Czech citizen present the following: I arrived in Italy (Regno) on August 16, 1939 with the intention of staying for three or four weeks, for pleasure and recreation and then I wanted to emigrate to the United Kingdom, where my son resided at the time and in such conditions that would have allowed him to pay for my "entrance" in the country. My luggage had already been sent to England and the ticket to London (through Paris) had been bought and paid for. All the documents required to enter the United Kingdom were ready and I had already talked to the British ambassador in Florence, who will be able to confirm that I have been added to his list in August 1939; however, the start of the war made my journey to the United Kingdom impossible.

Moreover, my name appears on the waiting list of the American Consulate in Naples, as shown in the letter here attached and sent to the Florence Police Headquarters, since March 3. I already have all the documents needed to enter the United States. The money I have received, comes from both the United States and the United Kingdom. Currently, even with all my effort, I would not be able to go anywhere else, but I am certain that, eventually, I will obtain the visum either for the United Kingdom or the United States. I am a single woman, a widow and I am currently living in the Balestri Pension, in Florence, in Piazza Mentana, living therefore a respectful and decent life: I am asking for the right to stay in Italy until I receive the permission to move to another country.

Respectfully,

Clara Buchsbaum

P.S. My health has also been getting worse lately.

1941: "Persecution of Jews in Italy" (Origin of document unknown)

Klara (Clara) Babad, of Sigmund, widow of Ignatz Buchsbaum, was born in July 1882, in Bielsko. She had first arrived in Italy on

August 16, 1939 for pleasure and recreation, staying at the Balestri Pension in Piazza Mentana, Florence, with no relatives.

Clara's intention was to stay in Italy for three or four weeks and then emigrate to England, where her son was residing at the time.

She was registered in the British Consulate in Florence, she had her ticket and she had sent her luggage through Paris, yet, in the end, she was not allowed to leave Italy because the war had started. Starting 3 March of the previous year, Clara had sent a request to the American consulate in Prague to be added to the *waiting list,* to emigrate to the United States, in order to meet up with another son, who resided in Philadelphia.[1] She had passport n. 546, given to her by the Police Department of Morava Ostrova on November 27, 1936, then renewed in June 1939 with an expiration date of November 6, 1941.

After her arrival in Italy, Clara was granted a six-month stay, until February 15, 1940. As the American Consulate in Naples was not granting Clara the VISA to enter the United States, she asked to extend her stay in Italy and, in order to do so, her son, Ben, from the United States, had to intervene.

The Minister of the Interior was informed of the situation by a member of Parliament, Alessandroni, "an Italian-American of great prestige," judge of the Court of Appeal, informed by another member of Parliament himself.

At the end of January, Clara was granted the extension of her stay in Italy, while waiting for her VISA to enter the United States. However, on 18 July, Clara was included in the list of Jewish women residing in Florence, therefore she was interned in Frosinone and then arrived in San Donato on August 28. Starting February 1941 Clara started asking for a subsidy, as she was no longer receiving financial help from abroad. She asked for permission to go to the American Consulate in Rome, where she was supposed to undergo a medical exam, first in April 1941 and then again in June 1943.

Clara also asked that the Podestà (a chief magistrate in a Medieval Italian municipality) was authorized to return the passport. From July 2 to 26, 1941 she was in Rome, waiting for the ferry ticket that her son was supposed to send from the United States.

Then, on 27 July she went back to San Donato. The second time, it was Delasem, in the Spring of 1943, that asked for the authorization to send Clara to Rome, in order to finalize the details of her emigration request. The organization stated that Clara owned "an invitation from the Consulate and a ferry ticket."

Yet, in the end, her destiny was just like the one of other Jews. She was arrested and deported and she arrived in Auschwitz on May 23, 1944.

Most likely she was assigned a serial number, unknown to this day, and she passed away right after her arrival to the concentration camp in May.

John E. Buchsbaum   804 West 180th Street
                                     New York City
                                     August 2, 1941.

Mr. Murray LeVine
c/o HIAS
330 South 9th Street
Philadelphia Pa.

Dear Mr. LeVine:-

        I have just been informed that the State Dept.
accepts again visa-applications in behalf of persons
residing in Italy. Would you please be kind enough to
send me 2 sets of affidavit-forms to enable me to apply
for my Mother who is in Italy. The guarantors for my Mother
are my cousin Mrs. Benjamin Buchsbaum and myself.

        Mrs. Buchsbaum is on vacation now and I shall
mail the completed form to her to be signed. I have all
supporting documents here so that there will be no delay
in filing of the application.

        I would appreciate it very much if you would send
me two more sets of affidavit-forms for a friend of mine
whose parents are in the same position as my Mother. Please
send therefore 4 sets of affidavit forms.

        I would prefer to come to Philadelphia to fill in
and to sign the applications in your presence if it should
be necessary to do it in the presence of an official of
a refugee organization, as it takes weeks to get an appoint-
ment at the HIAS in New York. I shall probably phone you
on Monday morning to get your reply as soon as possible.

        I thank you for your kindness and remain

                    very sincerely yours

**1941: Letter to the Hebrew Immigrant Aid Society
(HIAS) from John Buchsbaum requesting paperwork
leading to immigration for Clara Buchsbaum**

MUNICIPALITY OF S. DONATO VAL DI COMINO

Province   of   Frosinone

*   *   *

After having inspected the County Council' s books

THE MAYOR CERTIFIES

that Mrs. Clara BUCHSBAUM received as a civil internee, the subsidy as of 1st March 1941 up to the end of 1943.

This Certificate has been issued on usual paper for all lawful purposes.

THE MAYOR

sged: (Antonio Cedrone)

Certification for subsidy for Clara Buchsbaum for 1941-1943 by the municipality of San Donato Val Di Comino

One of four postcards written by Clara Buchsbaum from San Donato to her brother Norbert Babad in Ostrava in 1942 and 1943

Four postcards appeared in my email in March 2020, sent by Radan Salomonovič of the Czech Republic, a philatelist, who recognized the Buchsbaum name. The postcards had been put up for sale not relating to content but for the stamps and postmarks.

Mr. Salomonovič, son of the late Michal Salomonovič who escorted my sons and me around Ostrava in 2008, facilitates information gathering by descendants of the Jewish community of Ostrava.

September 1957: Affidavit submitted by John Buchsbaum seeking reparations from the German government (English translation)

Affidavit

In full knowledge of the importance of an affidavit, I, the signer John Hans Buchsbaum, residing at 245 Mather Road, Jenkintown, Pennsylvania, U.S.A., declare the following in place of an oath.

My mother, Mrs. Klara Buchsbaum, was born on July 1, 1882, in Bielitz, Silesia, Austria-Hungary, as the daughter of the bookkeeper Sigmund Babad and his wife Jeanette Babad, nee Reitman. Her religion was Judaism. She attended German elementary – and middle – schools in Bielietz and her mother tongue was German.

On February 7, 1906, my mother married my father, Mr. Ignatz Buchsbaum, bookseller in Maehrisch-Ostrau-Oderfurt, in Austria-Hungary, later Czechoslovakia. As a result, my parents received the Czechoslovak citizenship. Out of their union, two children were born. My sister, Grete, later married Spitzer, born on February 12, 1907, and I, Hans (John) Buchsbaum, born on December 24, 1910. My sister Grete, her husband Dr. Ing. Hugo Spitzer and their only daughter Susie were deported to Lublin in 1941 and have since been missing. After the war, they were reported dead.

From the beginning of my parents' marriage until my father's death on August 27, 1937, my mother worked in my father's company and contributed to establishing the I. Buchsbaum company, Maehr. Ostrau-Privoz, as the largest German publisher and distributor of books. Any German publisher, operating before the war, could have attested the importance of our company. Our company was a member of the stock market organization of German book sellers in Leipzig and the organization of German book sellers in Aussig a.E., Czechoslovkia. In the year of 1913, my mother received her diploma as a book seller. She was an employee of the company until she became a co-owner with me in 1937 after my father's death.

After my father's death on August 27, 1937, my mother, Mrs. Klara Buchsbaum, inherited 50% of the company I. Buchsbaum, and I inherited the remaining 50%. My sister Grete Spitzer, nee Buchsbaum, received her part of the inheritance in cash and in treasury bills.

The company that my mother and I headed as co-owners had a value of approximately 300.000 Kc. In 1938.

In order to confirm this information, I provide the following witnesses:
Mr. Dr. Leo Spitzer, 45 East End Avenue, New York, N.Y., who was involved in the handling of the inheritance. An affidavit will be provided.

Mr. Ferdinand Schindler, Heidelberg-Pfaffengrund, Am Heimgarten 6, who had been employed in our company for 20 years and who remained in the company when it was obtained by the German authorities (there are a few words missing at the bottom of the page).

Shortly after the invasion of German troops in the March of 1939, four men appeared in our company who presented themselves as part of the Gestapo. We were forbidden to enter the property of our company or to withdraw any amount from our company accounts. Shortly thereafter, Mr. Erwin Hruschka, a former employee of our company, was installed as the acting director.

My mother and I had in the meantime applied for American visas. In order to receive the permit to leave, we each had to deposit 200.000 Kc (together 400.000 Kc) at the tax office in Maehr.Ostrau as a security deposit for future taxes. In addition, my mother was forced to transfer all her mobile and non-mobile assets without fail to the Boehmische Escompte Bank and Credit Union in Prague for "management" according to the non-Arian asset rules.

On a Sunday morning in May 1939, I was warned by an acquaintance in the Ostrauer police headquarters to leave the city before Monday morning in order to avoid my pending arrest. The same afternoon, I went to Prague, from there to London, England, where I arrived in June 1939 without any funds. From England, I then emigrated in February 1941 to the United States.

My mother couldn't at first decide to leave her home and her life's work and staid in Maehr.Ostrau. Shortly after my departure, she wrote to me from Lorence, Italy, that the Gestapo had asked about me when they couldn't find me and had left making threats. My mother who then feared for her life had taken advantage of the opportunity of the release of Italian currency funds for travelers in order to flee to Italy in July. My attempt to bring my mother to England was destroyed with the outbreak of the war. After Italy entered the war, I found out through Switzerland that my mother had been interned in San Donato, Frosinone, Val die Comino. She had no financial means and lived on the small amounts of money that friends from Switzerland and Italy had transferred to her.

After my emigration to the United States in February 1941, I sent my mother whatever I could spare from my meager income. My efforts to bring her to the United States failed again when America entered the war. From that time on, I only received two messages (letters?) through the Red Cross and a letter from a friend in Switzerland stating that my mother lived in great misery and asking me to send money to her through him. From that time on, I no longer received any news about her. After the war, I found out that my mother had been deported by the German authorities to Auschwitz where she lost her precious life in the gas chamber.

I also found out after the war that our company had been sold in 1941 by the German authorities to a Mr. Paul Apelt for Kc 803.655.45, documented in a copy of a letter from the district administrator of the higher court in Maehr. Ostrau. Neither my mother, nor I had been informed or consulted. In addition, my mother and I never received any amount of money or other values from this sale. The enclosed copy of the letter by the district administrator of the higher court was sent to me in 1946 by my lawyer in Maehr.Ostrau, Dr. Norbert Babad. I had never received the original and can therefore not provide you with a notarized copy. However instead of an oath, I declare that the enclosed copy of 1946 is the exact copy of the original letter that Dr. Norbert Babad had received.

Since my sister, Grete Spitzer, nee Buchsbaum, and her daughter Susie Spitzer passed away before my mother's death, I was recognized as my mother's sole inheritor by the administration in Maehr.Ostrau after the war.

Sworn and subscribed before me this   day of July, 1963.

1996: Deportation and extermination notification for the Spitzer family obtained from the International Red Cross

FEDERACE ŽIDOVSKÝCH OBCÍ V ČESKÉ REPUBLICE

Maiselova 18
P.O.B. 297
110 01 Praha 1

V Praze dne

ÚSTŘEDNÍ KARTOTÉKA — TRANSPORTY:

R. č. 116600

S p i t z e r o v á Greta

Rodná data: 12.2.1907

Adresa před: M.Ostrava Střelnice 24

1. transport	2. transport
dne: 30. IX. 1942	dne: 5.10.1942
	číslo: Bt-918
Bm č. 583	do: † Treblinky

FEDERACE ŽIDOVSKÝCH OBCÍ
ČESKÉ REPUBLICE
Praha 1, Maiselova

133

ÚSTŘEDNÍ KARTOTÉKA — TRANSPORTY

R. č. 116615

S p i t z e r o v á Zuzana

Rodná data: 6.3.1931

Adresa před deportaci: M.Ostrava Střelnice 24

1. transport	2. transport
dne: 30. IX. 1942	dne: 5.10.1942
Bm	číslo: Bt-919
č. 584	do: † Treblinky
I.	

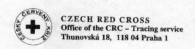

CZECH RED CROSS
Office of the CRC – Tracing service
Thunovská 18, 118 04 Praha 1

~ 2 5 1997

American Red Cross
The Holocaust & War Victims
Tracing & Informat.Center
4700 Mount Hope Drive
Baltimore,Maryland 21215-3231
U.S.A.

YOUR REF.	OUR REF.	PRAGUE
ISS-H-22583	128509/Hol	13 March 1997

Re: SPITZER Hugo, Gretel, Susi

Inq.: Barbara Gilford

Dear Red Cross colleague:

Referring to your inquiry we would like to advise we have been able to ascertain only following information about the individuals:

SPITZER Hugo, born 22.4.1899, last known address: Moravská Ostrava, Střelnice 24, was deported 30.9.1942 to Terezin with the transport Bm – 582 and then 5.10.1942 to Treblinka with the transport Bt – 917.
With regard to SPITZEROVÁ Greta and Zuzana, we have the same information. Enclosed we are sending the verified copies of the record from the card-index of deported persons, which we received from the Jewish institution in Prague.

Yours sincerely

Ivana Holubová
Head of Tracing Service
CZECH RED CROSS

Encl.ment.

Telephone:
(42 2) 24510220 27266204
Fax:
(42 2)

Telegrams:
CROIX Praha

Telex:
122400 csrc c

135

2018: Left to right: Andrew Gilford, Barbara Gilford, Shari (David's wife) and David Gilford, visiting San Donato

The generations continue

Andrew Gilford, his wife Debra, son Asher and daughter Elia

1. This translated document states that Clara was intending to join "another son" in Philadelphia, and the document names this "son" as Ben Buchsbaum. Clara's only son was my father Hans (John). Ben Buchsbaum was a cousin, not a son. It is unclear whether this represents an intentional misstatement on Clara's part, or whether there was an error of transcription at the time the document was drafted for Clara.

ABOUT THE AUTHOR

Barbara Gilford began as an educator and later maintained a clinical practice in psychotherapy for almost twenty-five years before writing *Heart Songs -A Holocaust Memoir*. Her MSW degree from Wurzweiler School of Social Work, Yeshiva University, formalized her lifelong quest to understand how people work out their lives. Trauma, loss and suffering in her clients engendered in her deep appreciation for the strength and resilience embedded in the human psyche and spirit.

The author contributed more than two hundred articles on dance to The New York Times, *New Jersey Weekly* section and won two awards for her journalism. Barbara is an accomplished presenter who has told her family's story in high schools, colleges, synagogues, centers for Holocaust studies, book clubs, and community organizations.

In addition to writing, Barbara reads and immerses herself in film, classical music, ballet and Broadway. She enjoys art museums, European travel and also her home in Morris County, New Jersey.

The author is available for book talks and presentations.

Readers can communicate with the author through her website at www.barbaragilford.com.

ACKNOWLEDGMENTS

My world is graced by many people who have been part of this particular journey and of other endeavors throughout the decades of my life. Both streams have run parallel and also merged in places. I feel so fortunate to have travelled through the years with the following cherished people and extend to them my most heartfelt gratitude.

Liesbeth Heenk, my publisher, you have been such a delight to work with. You are the one who miraculously told me, "Yes, I will publish your book." You have provided literary support and a pathway to publication, and your efforts to arrange a translation into Italian have expanded the reach of my story.

Lorraine Ash, my literary editor and coach, you believed in my book from the first chapter and have continued to affirm my writing. I extend my deepest gratitude to you.

Kerstin White translated my grandmother's letters with deep respect and dedication. You gave me my grandmother's voice and her heart. Your translation made possible the writing of this book and has forged a treasured friendship between us.

David and Shari Gilford, my son and daughter-in-law, you have seen me through computer crises with patience and with such generosity of time and energy. Your literary feedback has always been sensitive, and very astute. I am filled with gratitude for both of you. *Heart Songs* has reached fruition because of your involvement.

My son Andrew Gilford and his wife Debra Bufton listen, support, advise, and comfort me at every turn. First among your many accomplishments are the two very fine children you have birthed and raised.

Angela West, a Ph.D. candidate at Drew University and Coordinator of the Center for Holocaust/Genocide Study, has utilized her extensive knowledge of history in helping to prepare this memoir for publication. Angela's expertise on the Holocaust, sense of aesthetics, and her appreciation of the nuances of language and writing have made her an invaluable assistant.

Rachael Wolensky, a tech editor without match, visited me on many Saturdays to align text, insert photos, scan documents, and clean up errors in spacing. I have greatly valued your patience and assistance.

Robert Ready, Ph.D., Professor Emeritus of English, and the lead writing instructor for the Jacqueline Berke Legacy Writing Workshops for Children of Holocaust Survivors at the Drew University Center for Holocaust/Genocide Study, provided inspiration and affirmation. In each class session you created opportunities for deeper exploration of the legacy of the participants and in the process came healing.

Grace Cohen Grossmann and Fred Wasserman of the United States Holocaust Memorial Museum facilitated my donation of all the original Buchsbaum family materials. Thank you for giving my family papers a home in the museum archives.

With deepest appreciation to these special people in San Donato Val di Comino, Italy: Delia Roffo provided simultaneous translation during our visit to San Donato. This book could not have been written without your prodigious effort. Mayor Enrico Pittiglio welcomed us warmly with gifts and a special breakfast. Luca Leone, historian of San Donato, provided important information about my grandmother and the final round-up by the German soldiers. Alfonsa Gaudiello carried memories of my Oma Clara for more than seventy years and shared them with so much affection. I carry all of you in my heart.

To my friends and fellow writers Jeanne D'Haem and Eric Barr of the Temple Sinai Writers' Circle I send gratitude for all the feedback, patience and the comfort you provided as I wrote about my family and grieved my loss of them.

I will never forget Michal and Libuše Salomonovič of Ostrava. Libuše co-authored *Ostrava and Its Jews: Now No One Sings You Lullabies* and helped me and many others trace our family's lives in pre-war Ostrava. Sadly, Michal lost his battle with cancer in the summer of 2019. Their son Radan continues to facilitate the acquisition of information for many descendants of the Jews of Ostrava.

Dr. Eva Vogel translated a high school research paper about my cousin Susi Spitzer from Czech into English which provided new information. I would like to thank Ludovica Gioacchini, for translations from Italian.

Hana Sustkova, Ph.D., head of Vitkovice, Jsc, Company Archive and researcher in the Center for Economic and Social History, University of Ostrava, and co-author of *Ostrava and Its Jews: Now No One Sings You Lullabies,* read my manuscript and offered corrections and additional information. She also translated information on the Buchsbaum family.

David Lawson, Ph.D., co-author of *Ostrava and Its Jews: Now No One Sings You Lullabies,* provided generous feedback and information.

My deep gratitude to Marion Wiesel for giving me permission to use the quote from Elie Wiesel which captures the themes of my book. My appreciation is also extended to Olivia Crvaric, Project Manager at the Elie Wiesel Foundation, who facilitated my request and Mrs. Wiesel's permission.

My gratitude can never match the enduring gifts of friendship from all of my many friends, some of whom are also writers. They have encouraged and supported me through this journey and through life. Marianne Avery; Eve Baruch; my dear cousin Paul Bellet; Jean Bohn; Lucy Castles; Carolyn DeCastro; Mimi Eddleman; Tilly-Jo Emerson; Diane Finch; Donna Clair Gasiewicz; Brigitte Heffernan; Donna Kahn; Sara Kushnir; Maureen Kennedy; Helen Lippman; Joan MacCoy; Susan Mimnaugh; Michelle Mongey; Regie Buchsbaum Roth; Mim Smith; Susan Skovronek; the late Barbara Shalit; Barbara Hicks Shapiro; Sue Soriano; Ida Welsh, and Dawn Woodward. Thank you for your continuing presence in my life. You have sustained me and we will continue our conversations into the beyond.

For the late Ann Buchsbaum who got on a Kindertransport from Vienna to Holland and never stopped going. You inspired me, you encouraged me from the time I was fifteen years old, and you said at some point: "Isn't it time you wrote a book?" Your love and friendship contributed significantly to the person I am today.

And for my mother, Eleanor, you loved me until the end of your life like no other, and only wanted me to be happy. Your wishes came true.

Made in the USA
Coppell, TX
26 September 2021